PAKISTAN'S ECONOMY AND TRADE IN THE AGE OF GLOBAL VALUE CHAINS

JANUARY 2022

Co-publication of the Asian Development Bank and Islamic Development Bank Institute.

معهد البنك الإسلامي للتنمية
Islamic Development Bank Institute

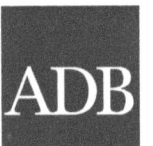

ADB

CONTENTS

TABLES, FIGURES, AND BOXES

Boxes

FOREWORD

Over the last 30 years, the world has witnessed a dramatic expansion of cross-border production networks known as global value chains (GVCs). Participation in these networks has boosted economic growth of many developing countries, especially in Asia. The extent of economies' participation in GVCs has also determined the relative impact of such diverse elements as technological progress, economic policies, international politics, and even the coronavirus disease (COVID-19). Despite this, data scarcity has left the GVC phenomenon understudied, particularly its impact on developing countries like Pakistan. The Asian Development Bank (ADB) and the Islamic Development Bank (IsDB) have been collaborating to bridge this analytical gap and to support evidence-based decision-making.

This report uses traditional and modern statistics—including the multiregional input–output tables (MRIOTs) compiled by ADB—and cutting-edge analytical methods to understand how the various facets of the GVC phenomenon impact Pakistan. One of the key outputs of the ADB–IsDB collaboration is the timely production of high-quality country-specific supply-use tables. These tables are essential for the compilation of an MRIOT that accurately depicts the local and cross-border production and trade linkages, and consumption and investment patterns. ADB's MRIOT is unique among intercountry input–output tables in that it includes supply-use details for Pakistan and data to the year 2020, critical for analyzing the economic impact of COVID-19. Through their research on and operations in Pakistan, ADB and IsDB have built considerable institutional knowledge that has served to enhance the quality and utility of this current study.

Pakistan has made significant economic progress and achieved considerable poverty reduction since the turn of the millennium. Yet, the country is still one of the few relatively large and diverse economies whose participation in international trade—and hence in GVCs—has remained well below its potential. In a first for Pakistan, this report estimates and analyzes the key economic indicators essential for a deeper and comprehensive understanding of the GVC phenomenon in the country. Based on statistical analysis, the study also indicates the GVC segments that Pakistan could enter and, consequently, move up the value chains. Topical subjects with implications for the country's GVC participation, such as regional integration, agglomeration, and COVID-19, are also discussed. The report concludes with a synopsis of the broad strategies successfully adopted by countries leading to their GVC participation.

We anticipate that this study will be an excellent reference for policymakers, development practitioners, government officials, researchers, students, and others who would benefit from a deeper understanding of Pakistan's GVC involvement. We would like to congratulate the ADB and IsDB officials, along with the consultants working on this collaboration, for producing this important statistical analysis, which will certainly facilitate evidence-based policymaking.

Joseph Ernest Zveglich, Jr.
Acting Chief Economist
Economic Research and
Regional Cooperation Department
Asian Development Bank

Sami Al-Suwailem
Acting Director General, Islamic Development
Bank Institute and Chief Economist,
Islamic Development Bank Group

ACKNOWLEDGMENTS

This report is part of an ongoing collaboration between the Asian Development Bank (ADB) and the Islamic Development Bank (IsDB) in providing knowledge solutions to key socioeconomic issues of Pakistan's participation in global value chains (GVCs). It employs well-structured economic data coupled with innovative analytical tools to describe the positioning of Pakistan in GVCs, the lengths of its GVC production, its patterns of specialization, and the price competitiveness of its exports, among many others. The key data source of this report is the ADB multiregional input–output (MRIO) database, the only time series of intercountry input–output tables to date that not only includes Pakistan but also has (preliminary) data for 2020. Given that it identifies key trends in Pakistan's GVC participation, this study would certainly serve as a useful reference for policymakers and analysts.

We gratefully acknowledge ADB's vice-president for Knowledge Management and Sustainable Development, Bambang Susantono; the IsDB's vice-president for Country Programs, Mansur Muhtar; and acting director general of IsDB Institute and chief economist of IsDB Group, Sami Al-Suwailem—they provided strong leadership and indispensable guidance from the start to undertake this study. We also thank Edimon Ginting and Joseph Ernest Zveglich, Jr. of ADB; and Kadir Basboga, Abu Camara, Mohamed Elgoussi, Ahmad Zafarullah Abdul Jalil, Novia Budi Parwanto, Ali Rashed, Abdul Rashid, and Bukhari M. S. Sillah of IsDB Institute for providing valuable support for the overarching initiative to develop quality statistics and analysis to discern the phenomenon of economic globalization.

This report was written by Kenneth Anthony Luigi Reyes under the direct supervision of Mahinthan Joseph Mariasingham, with inputs from Julian Thomas Alvarez, Ridhima Bahl, Ma. Charmaine Crisostomo, Janine De Vera, Christian Regie Jabagat, Leila Rahnema, Marcus Jude San Pedro, and Eric Suan. The ADB MRIO database is consolidated and maintained by a core team comprising Michael John Barsabal, John Arvin Bernabe, Janine De Vera, Julieta Magallanes, Sarah Mae Manuel, and Ana Francesca Rosales. We also acknowledge the Joint Research Centre of the European Commission for sharing the industry and country data from the World Input–Output Database (WIOD).

Joy Quitazol-Gonzalez edited the publication. Joe Mark Ganaban led the typesetting process and cover design. Eric Suan organized and coordinated the preparation of this report. The publishing team in ADB's Department of Communications and Corporate Services Department Logistics Management Unit (Printing) provided general guidance on production issues.

Elaine S. Tan
Advisor, Office of the Chief Economist
and Director General, and Head,
Statistics and Data Innovation Unit,
Economic Research and Regional
Cooperation Department

Areef Suleman
Director
Economic Research and Statistics
Islamic Development Bank Institute

ABBREVIATIONS

ADB	Asian Development Bank
ASEAN	Association of Southeast Asian Nations
CAREC	Central Asia Regional Economic Cooperation
COVID-19	coronavirus disease
DAVAX	directly absorbed value-added exports
DVA	domestic value added
FCE	final consumption expenditure
FVA	foreign value added
GDP	gross domestic product
GVC	global value chain
HHI	Herfindahl-Hirschman Index
HS	Harmonized System
IOT	input–output table
IMF	International Monetary Fund
IsDB	Islamic Development Bank
ISIC	International Standard Industrial Classification
METI	Japan Ministry of Economy, Trade and Industry
MRIO	multiregional input–output
NAFTA	North American Free Trade Agreement
PDC	pure double-counting
PRC	People's Republic of China
RCA	revealed comparative advantage
RCI	regional concentration index
REER	real effective exchange rate
REF	reflection
REX	reexports
RTA	regional trade agreement
SAARC	South Asian Association for Regional Cooperation
SUT	supply–use table
VAX	value-added exports
WTO	World Trade Organization

HIGHLIGHTS

This statistical report examines the economy and trade of Pakistan in the context of global value chains (GVCs) during the period 2000–2020. It combines innovative analytical tools with the latest available data to produce indicators that describe facets of Pakistan's GVC participation, the lengths of its GVC production, its patterns of specialization, and the price competitiveness of its exports, among many others.

Overview of the Economy and Trade

- Pakistan has had an uneven growth experience. After an average annual gross domestic product (GDP) growth rate of 6.4% in the 1980s, its decade averages have since been below 5.0%. Many workers remain employed in low-productivity jobs in agriculture and the informal sector. Per capita GDP is similar to Bangladesh and Cambodia but is behind other developing countries in Asia and the Pacific like the Philippines and Viet Nam. Nevertheless, it is to Pakistan's credit that it has managed to cut poverty from 64% in 2001 to 24% in 2015 under national poverty lines.

- One viable strategy that Pakistan can adopt to boost its growth is to further open its economy to trade. At just 30%, Pakistan exhibits one of the lowest trade-to-GDP ratios in the world, even when taking its size into account. This indicates great potential for improvement. Studies have affirmed numerous benefits to economic openness, including opportunities for specialization, access to wider markets, the inflow of know-how, and the formalization of the economy.

- Existing patterns indicate that Pakistan's trade is currently oriented to the United States, Europe, and the People's Republic of China (PRC). It specializes in textiles, though some of its agricultural products are sold to the Middle East. Interestingly, it does not have a significant trading relationship with its proximate neighbors in South Asia.

- While the vast majority of its export products fall under the textiles grouping, formal measures of export concentration suggest that Pakistan's exports basket is relatively more diversified than other textiles-heavy exporters like Bangladesh and Cambodia. However, its exports are less diversified than its neighbor India.

Participation in Global Value Chains

- Decomposing the value-added origins and destinations of Pakistan's exports illuminates much about its participation in GVCs. It is found that a large portion of its exports fall under direct trading, the simplest kind of trade where value added solely from Pakistan is sent to and absorbed completely by the importing partner. In 2020, this amounted to $18.9 billion against gross exports of $24.0 billion. Indirect trading involves foreign value added entering into countries' production, a form of cross-border production-sharing that characterize GVCs. In 2020, Pakistan's indirect trading amounted to $5.8 billion.

- Decomposing trade by value added reveals indirect trading relationships that are masked by conventional trade data. Some 15.8% of Pakistan's exports that would undergo reexporting made their first landing in the PRC. Bangladesh also gets a prominent role, receiving 7.8% of exports that would undergo reexporting. On the other hand, some 17.4% of the imported inputs embedded in Pakistan's exports came from the PRC, followed by 12.8% that came from the United States.

- Quantifying the importance of GVCs is the GVC participation rate. Two approaches are possible: (i) a trade-based approach, which looks at the share of indirect trading in exports; and (ii) a production-based approach, which looks at the share of domestic value added (i.e., GDP) that is exported in an unfinished state. Pakistan's GVC participation rates are low. While other developing countries, notably Viet Nam and Cambodia, have greatly expanded their GVC engagement since 2000, Pakistan's rates have stayed within a tight range over the course of 2 decades. At the sector level, water transport services and metals had the highest participation rates, though textiles remained the largest in terms of the absolute level of GVC-related exports.

- Another way to characterize GVCs is to measure their lengths. Any given firm may be positioned in its value chain by measuring, on the one hand, the number of stages separating its output from final consumers (also known as the forward production length) and, on the other, the number of stages separating its output from the primary inputs (or the backward production length). Total GVC length for Pakistan was 7.58 stages in 2000, rising to 8.03 in 2010, then rising more modestly to 8.18 by 2020. Across sectors, the general conclusion is that lengths increased between 2000 and 2010 but decreased between 2010 and 2020.

- Decomposing forward lengths suggests that Pakistan exports relatively simple types of textile products, relying on foreign processing—about 2.09 stages in 2020—to produce the finished goods that reach consumers. Exports of agricultural products, meanwhile, undergo both domestic (2.26 stages) and foreign (2.09 stages) processing.

Specialization and Competitiveness

- The concept of comparative advantage is operationalized by the revealed comparative advantage (RCA) index, a ratio that compares the share of a sector in a given country's exports to the average share of that sector across all countries. An RCA index of greater than 1 indicates a comparative advantage in that sector. Using GVC-adjusted measures, Pakistan heavily specializes in textiles (RCA of 10.2) and agriculture (RCA of 6.4). It registered very low RCA indexes for the manufacturing sectors.

- A question arises on where along these value chains Pakistan is finding its niche: in the upstream sections (closer to primary producers), the downstream sections (closer to final consumers), or somewhere in the middle? The GVC position index suggests that the top textiles-specializing countries were in the downstream end, and Pakistan was no exception. It tended to use designs from abroad to produce textile products that, with little further processing, went straight to final consumers. In contrast, Pakistan was the only one in the upstream region among the agriculture-specializing countries, suggesting that its products undergo plenty of further processing abroad before final consumption.

- The real effective exchange rate (REER) is a price index that measures changes in a country's price competitiveness relative to its trade competitors. If the REER goes up, then the country's prices have gone up relative to its competitors; thus, it is said to have lost competitiveness. Likewise, if the REER goes down, then it has gained competitiveness.

- Pakistan's REER indexes for textiles and agriculture are strongly correlated, with both experiencing high appreciation in 2011 and modest depreciation in 2018–2019. This may be concerning since it implies little diversification in Pakistan's export competitiveness. Moreover, the modest depreciation the two sectors registered in 2018–2019 were overshadowed by a much larger depreciation in the aggregate REER, suggesting a boost in overall competitiveness that appears to have been dampened by Pakistan's largest sectors.

- Countries are generally advised to try and aim for stable currencies. Measuring volatility by the standard deviation in changes in the REER index over 2010–2019, Pakistan's 8.3 points was one of the highest among the countries and economies included in the Asian Development Bank (ADB) Multiregional Input–Output (MRIO) database. It is more volatile than countries like Bangladesh, Cambodia, Sri Lanka, and Viet Nam. This makes any effort to expand its external sector more challenging.

Other Topics in Global Value Chains

- As globalization picked up pace in the 1990s, so did initiatives to deepen and regulate trade on a regional basis. Beginning in the 1980s, the countries of South Asia began to abandon the import substitution policies they had followed since independence in favor of trade liberalization, establishing the South Asian Association for Regional Cooperation (SAARC) in 1985 to promote dialogue. Through the SAARC, the South Asian Preferential Trade Area was established in 1995 and expanded into the South

Asian Free Trade Area in 2006. Its members are Afghanistan, Bangladesh, Bhutan, India, Maldives, Nepal, Pakistan, and Sri Lanka. Elsewhere, Pakistan has also been an active member of the Central Asia Regional Economic Cooperation (CAREC) Program, which focuses on regional investments and policy initiatives.

- The regional concentration index (RCI) quantifies the extent of regional integration using value-added-adjusted trade flows, where an index of greater than 1 implies the region's members are trading with each other more than expected. By this measure, the SAARC bloc is less integrated than other blocs like the Association of Southeast Asian Nations, the European Union, and the North American Free Trade Agreement.

- Regional integration may also be visualized with a skyline chart, which represents each sector as a "tower" whose width is its share in the region's output and whose height is its output expressed as a share of the portion induced by domestic demand. Its main purpose is to show where the region is self-sufficient in, these being the sectors for which its own internal demand is enough to exhaust its output. The skyline chart for SAARC makes evident the economic structure of its members, with a large share attributable to agriculture for which the region is just about self-sufficient. Its most export-oriented sector is unsurprisingly textiles, for which output is 1.5 times the amount the region demands. The SAARC's manufacturing demand is generally dependent on imports, with its output in metals, electricals, transport equipment, and other machinery meeting just 80% of its own demand.

- Domestic linkages add a layer of complexity to a country's role in GVCs. Largely due to trade barriers, domestic linkages play a significant role in Pakistan. An agglomeration index that measures how much value added is sourced from and/or absorbed by domestic sectors relative to the rest of the world suggests that, on average, production in Pakistan generates more value added to domestic sectors compared to neighbors Bangladesh, India, the PRC, and Sri Lanka.

- Various combinations of high and low backward and forward agglomeration indexes give four distinct classes: reshoring, high agglomeration, low agglomeration, and domestic value-added generating. Focusing on the textiles sector, Pakistan, along with India, belongs to the high agglomeration class. This implies high backward and forward agglomeration in both countries' textiles sector.

- The coronavirus disease (COVID-19) pandemic that began in 2020 set off unprecedented disruptions to economic activity and trade. Preliminary data in the ADB MRIO database suggest an inverted-U relationship, where the size of the COVID-19 shock increases (that is, becomes more negative) the higher the GVC participation rate up to about 45%, after which the shock decreases the higher the participation rate. Pakistan fits the pattern as it had both a low GVC participation rate (25.4%) and a relatively mild COVID-19 shock (−2.8 points).

- Counterfactual analysis shows that different countries experienced different outcomes from GVCs. In Pakistan's case, the analysis suggests that without any trade, its pandemic-induced contraction would have been 0.5 percentage points larger, meaning GVCs had a dampening effect. The opposite is found for a country like Sri Lanka, where the presence of trade relative to no trade increases the size of its contraction.

Reaping the Benefits of Global Value Chain Involvement

- Having among the lowest GVC participation rates in the world, the Pakistan economy is primed to benefit enormously from adopting a more outward-oriented development strategy. Provided that it does so in a careful and deliberate manner, the country's already impressive achievements in poverty reduction can be pushed further. The following are some principles to keep in mind.

- **Diversification.** The key to managing many types of risk is diversification. In the case of GVCs, Pakistan would do well to diversify not just its export basket but also the markets it sells to. Specialization in textiles is not necessarily an unsound strategy, but Pakistan must ensure that within this sector, its firms are able to participate all along the productivity spectrum and are not stuck in low-value-added segments. While its trading partners seem diversified, a trade-to-GDP ratio of 30% implies that Pakistan's producers are in effect concentrated in a single market: its own. Greater trade participation, then, will in itself diversify the country's sources of demand.

- **Investing in people.** Apart from its worthy contribution to welfare, investing in human capital yields significant returns when paired with the opportunities provided by GVCs. The services sector is already a proven driver of poverty reduction in Pakistan, albeit through the informal economy. Such talent can be turned to more productive employment in the global business process outsourcing industry. Indeed, the experiences of India and the Philippines have shown that manufacturing need no longer be synonymous with an export-led development strategy.

- **Institutional support.** Institutions must be responsive to the temporary disruptions that arise from opening up to trade. Policies must be designed to ensure that no group suffers too great a drop in welfare and that all have a path to participating gainfully in the external sector. Moreover, since good policy design requires plenty of timely information, support must be given to data-collecting agencies.

- **Multilateral engagement.** Trade can only thrive in a stable, rules-based global environment where competition is as free and as fair as possible. As such, it is in Pakistan's interest to strengthen multilateral bodies like the World Trade Organization, the SAARC, and the CAREC. It must actively participate not only in crafting their rules but also in enforcing them. Moreover, Pakistan must continue to pursue new trade agreements through which it can lower barriers to trade, exchange information, and establish mutual trust.

- **Remembering the basics.** Beyond GVCs, the usual set of principles that promote a robust and dynamic economy must not be neglected. The population must be healthy and educated. Sustained investments in physical infrastructure and information and communication technologies are necessary. Financial markets must be inclusive and well-developed. There must be faith in an impartial court system dedicated to the rule of law. All these provide the foundations upon which long-term growth can be possible.

Chapter 1

INTRODUCTION

This statistical report examines the economy and trade of Pakistan in the context of global value chains (GVCs), a form of fragmented production that has affected everything from automobiles to vaccines. GVCs pose a unique analytical challenge since conventional trade statistics implicitly bundle together value added of different origins. Thus, exports of country A to country B may contain contributions from countries C, D, and E—relationships that would generally be hidden. This report disentangles and analyzes such relationships. It combines innovative analytical tools with the latest available data to produce indicators that describe Pakistan's rate of GVC participation, the lengths of its GVC production, its patterns of specialization, and the price competitiveness of its exports—among many others. The key data source of this report is the Multiregional Input–Output (MRIO) database of the Asian Development Bank (ADB), the only time series of intercountry input–output tables to date that not only includes Pakistan but also has (preliminary) data for 2020. Box 1 provides more information on this dataset. It is hoped that the insights this report presents will prove useful for policymakers and the general public.

Box 1: The Asian Development Bank Multiregional Input–Output Database

The Asian Development Bank (ADB) multiregional input–output (MRIO) database is a time series intercountry input–output tables maintained by a dedicated team in ADB. It is freely available at https://mrio.adbx.online.

Information on cross-sector linkages are provided for 62 countries and economies. A residual "rest of the world" entity is also included, allowing the table to capture the entirety of global flows.

The ADB MRIO database is an extended version of the World Input–Output Database, 2013 release. Each country or economy is divided into 35 sectors, based on Table A2 of Timmer et al. (2015). There are five final demand categories: household final consumption expenditure (FCE), nonprofit institutions serving households FCE, government FCE, gross fixed capital formation, and changes in inventories.

Officially published national supply-use tables (SUTs) and/or input–output tables (IOTs) serve as benchmarks in the construction of the ADB MRIO database. In each national SUT or IOT, sector and product classifications were harmonized to follow the 35 sectors, and whenever necessary, SUTs were transformed into IOTs following the industry technology transformation assumption discussed in the European Commission (2008).

Benchmark IOTs also serve as the base structure for producing time series of the ADB MRIO tables, using published estimates on gross output, gross value added, taxes-less-subsidies on products, imports, and exports sourced from national statistical agencies and central bank databases as control totals. The structure of imports and exports are based on bilateral trade data extracted from the United Nations COMTRADE Database and government trade and balance of payments statistics. Once the national IOTs are integrated into the MRIO database, accounts for the sectors of "rest of the world" are manually and systematically adjusted to ensure consistency with country–sector totals in the MRIO database.

continued on next page.

Box 1 *continued.*

The basic structure of each of MRIO table is given below. It is composed of

Z	=	a matrix of intermediates use,
Y	=	a matrix of final demand,
va	=	a vector of country-sector value added, and
x	=	a vector of output.

Read vertically, the table shows the purchases of each country-sector, distinguished between intermediate inputs and primary inputs, the latter also called value added.

Read horizontally, it shows the sales of each country-sector, distinguished between intermediate sales and final sales.

The market-clearing condition stipulates that total purchases and total sales for each country-sector must equal. This amount is total output.

A Schematic Representation of the ADB MRIO

		Country A	...	Rest of the world	Country A	...	Rest of the world	Total output
		c1 ... c35	...	c1 ... c35	f1 ... f5	...	f1 ... f5	
Country A	c1 ⋮ c35							
⋮	⋮			**Z**			**Y**	**x**
Rest of the world	c1 ⋮ c35							
Value added		**va**						
Total output		**x**						

Source: Asian Development Bank. Multiregional Input–Output Database (accessed 1 August 2021).

Sources:
European Commission. 2008. *Eurostat Manual of Supply, Use and Input-Output Tables.* Luxembourg: Office for Official Publications of the European Communities.
M. P. Timmer, E. Dietzenbacher, B. Los, R. Stehrer, and G. J. de Vries. 2015. An Illustrated User Guide to the World Input-Output Database: The Case of Global Automotive Production. *Review of International Economics.* 23 (3). pp. 575–605.
World Input-Output Database, 2013 Release.

The mountainous terrain of Pakistan has historically served as the western gate to the Indian subcontinent. Through it passed waves of migrants who contributed to the ethnic and cultural makeup of South Asia. The earliest civilization in the region—also among the earliest in the world—emerged along the Indus River Valley in the fourth millennium BCE. The Indo-Aryans came in the second millennium BCE, followed by Islam in the 11th century. The subcontinent was ruled by the British from the 19th century to 1947, after which it was partitioned into the Dominion of India and the Dominion of Pakistan, each becoming independent countries. In 1971, the latter split into present-day Pakistan and Bangladesh (Wolpert 2004; Stephens 1967). As of 2020, Pakistan has a population of 215 million, of which 44% are classified as urban.[1] It shares a border with Afghanistan, India, Iran, and the People's Republic of China.

The rest of this report is structured as follows. Chapter 2 provides an overview of Pakistan's economy and trade using traditional statistics. Recognizing their limitations in the context of GVCs, Chapter 3 introduces an array of indicators obtained from the literature that characterizes Pakistan's place in international production sharing. Chapter 4 draws further insights into Pakistan's specialization and competitiveness by refining two classic trade indicators to account for GVCs. A number of special topics are discussed in Chapter 5, including Pakistan's membership in the South Asian Association for Regional Cooperation, its patterns of domestic agglomeration, and its economic performance under the coronavirus disease (COVID-19) pandemic of 2020. Chapter 6 concludes with recommendations for maximizing the benefits of GVCs and minimizing their risks.

---

[1] Asian Development Bank. Key Indicators Database: Pakistan (accessed 13 September 2021).

Chapter 2
OVERVIEW OF ECONOMY AND TRADE

This chapter establishes some key facts about Pakistan's economy using traditional datasets, including the gross domestic product (GDP) and its growth rate, the share of trade in GDP, and export patterns as recorded in merchandise trade statistics. These data point to an economy of middling growth, with a relatively small external sector that specializes mostly in textile products. While illuminating, these insights do not take into account intersector linkages and flows of value added, phenomena that can more suitably be studied with input–output datasets. These will be covered in Chapter 3.

Pakistan has had an uneven growth experience (ADB 2020a, 2020b; World Bank 2020a), captured in the boom–bust pattern of Figure 2.1. Though the country saw some promising growth episodes, especially during 1980–1992 when annual growth was generally at 5.0%–6.0%, its overall record has been a series of stops and starts, triggered by global events. Thus, the momentum from 2001 to 2008 was cut short by the global financial crisis in 2009, while the momentum from 2010 to 2019 was cut short by the pandemic in 2020. Indeed, the contraction in 2020 was the first for the country since 1952 (World Bank 2020a). On top of this, growth rates on average have been lackluster. After an average annual growth rate of 6.4% in the 1980s, its decade averages have since been below 5.0%, with the 2010s in particular registering an average of just 3.5%. Forecasts from the International Monetary Fund (IMF) suggest that it will remain at this pace for the near future.

Figure 2.1: Real Gross Domestic Product Growth Rate, Pakistan, 1980–2026

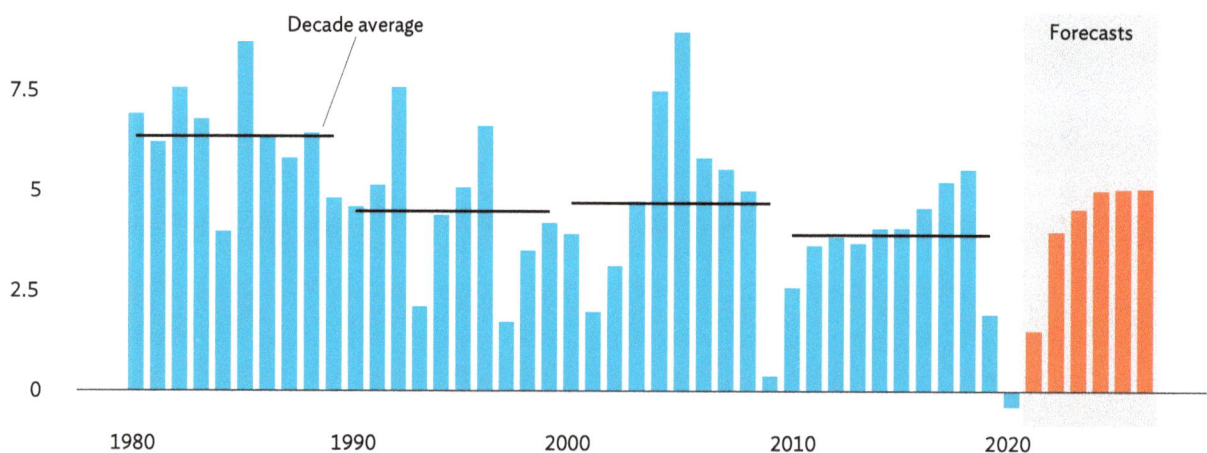

Notes: Years are fiscal years ending in 30 June. Forecasts are by the International Monetary Fund as of April 2021.
Source: International Monetary Fund. World Economic Outlook Database: April 2021 edition (accessed 1 August 2021).

World Bank (2020a) notes that private consumption, fueled by population growth and remittances, accounts for about 90% of growth. As demand outstrips domestic productive capacities, imports have persistently exceeded exports and have resulted in an unsustainable current account deficit. The low rate of private investment in both physical and human capital constrains Pakistan's growth potential to just 2.5%–3.0% per year (World Bank 2020a). Because the pace of structural transformation is sluggish, many workers remain employed in low-productivity jobs in the agriculture and informal services sectors.

Slower growth rates translate to slower improvements in the standard of living. Average real incomes, as measured by constant-price GDP per capita, increased by 64% between 1980 and 2000 and by 45% between 2000 and 2020. The average Pakistani was about 1.4 times better off in 2020 than in 1980. Adjusting for differences in price levels, Pakistan has about the same living standards as Bangladesh and Cambodia, but is behind other developing countries in Asia and the Pacific like the Philippines and Viet Nam. Nevertheless, it is to Pakistan's credit that it has managed to cut poverty from 64% in 2001 to 24% in 2015 under national poverty lines (World Bank 2020a). Sustained growth will carry such momentum forward.

One viable strategy that Pakistan can adopt to boost its growth is to further open its economy to trade. Many studies, including the paper by Frankel and Romer (1999), have affirmed that that trade more tend to grow faster. The four Asian Tigers—Hong Kong, China; the Republic of Korea; Singapore; and Taipei,China—had famously used an export-oriented development strategy to become advanced economies by the 1990s (Stiglitz 1996), an approach that is now being followed by Viet Nam and Cambodia, among others. Benefits to economic openness include opportunities for specialization, access to wider markets, and the inflow of investments, technology, and know-how. There is also evidence that trade promotes the reallocation of labor from the informal to the formal sector (McCaig and Pavcnik 2018). And whereas it was once thought that industrialization was the primary objective of openness, the experiences of India and the Philippines point to the possibility of services trade being a catalyst for growth as well (Chatterjee and Subramanian 2020; Thomas 2019).

In this regard, Figure 2.2 shows that Pakistan has a lot of room for improvement. Using statistics from 2019 (since 2020 was an unusual year), the scatterplot provides a snapshot of economic openness across various levels of GDP for 166 countries and economies with available data. At just 30%, Pakistan exhibits one of the lowest trade-to-GDP ratios in the world, measured as the sum of exports and imports divided by GDP. It is less open than neighbors India (39%) and Bangladesh (37%). Among the sample, it is only more open than Ethiopia, Brazil, and Sudan. While its present ratio is higher than the 15%–20% it registered in the 1960s–1970s, it is down from the peaks it saw in the 1990s when it reached 38%.

Figure 2.2: Trade Openness at Various Levels of Economic Development, 2019

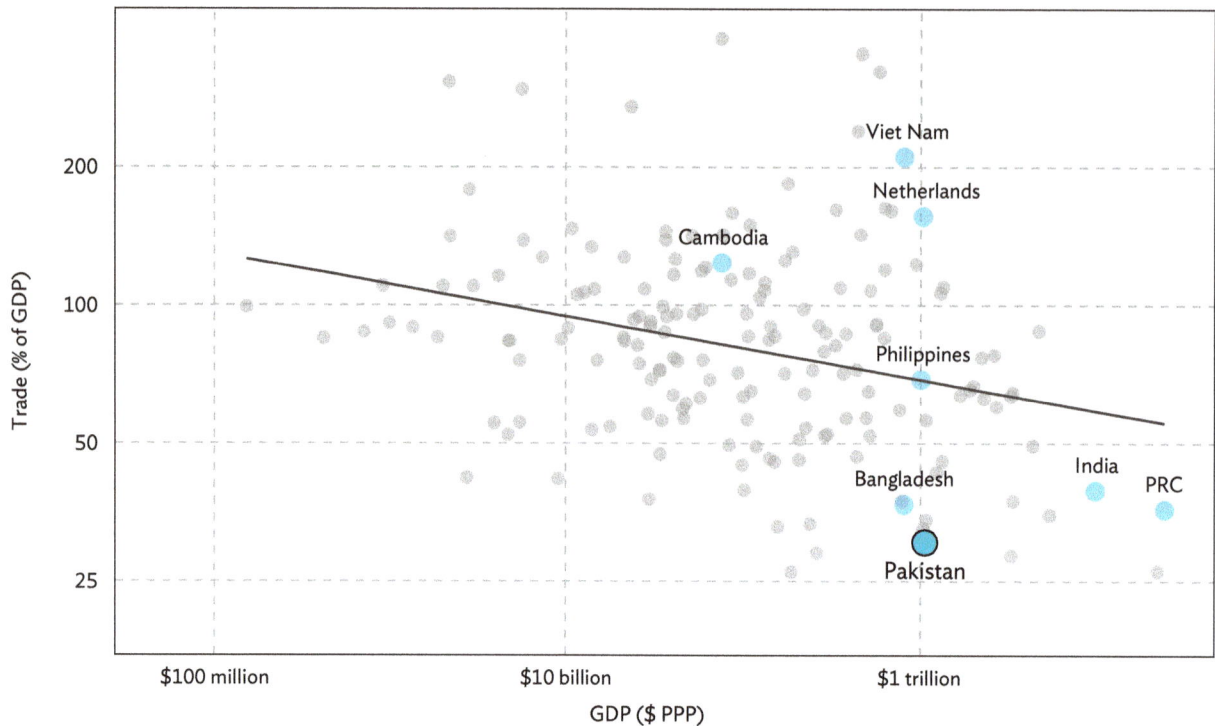

GDP = gross domestic product, PPP = purchasing power parity, PRC = People's Republic of China.
Notes: Horizontal axis is gross domestic product in current international dollars at PPP. Vertical axis is the sum of exports and imports of goods and services as a share of GDP.
Source: World Bank. World Development Indicators (accessed 1 August 2021).

The scatterplot highlights an inverse relationship between economic size and openness, with bigger countries tending to have smaller trade-to-GDP ratios. This is unsurprising since with size comes more opportunities to buy from and sell to domestic markets. Sitting at the 13th percentile of the sample by size, Pakistan is a relatively large country. However, even with this taken into account, its openness remains remarkably low. For example, countries that have GDPs comparable to that of Pakistan but with much higher trade-to-GDP include the Philippines (69%), the Netherlands (156%), and Viet Nam (210%). India's GDP is almost 10 times larger than Pakistan's, yet trade plays a greater role in its economy.

Figure 2.3 visualizes international trading networks as of 2019 and Pakistan's place in them. As it utilizes the United Nations Commodity Trade Statistics Database (UN Comtrade), as processed by CEPII's BACI International Trade Database,[2] only merchandise trade is included. Each node is a country or economy, positioned so as to group together those with significant mutual trade. For visual clarity, the figure only draws a trading link if the importing node is among the three largest importers of the exporting node. Node sizes are proportional to the number of such links the node is connected to. Thus, the fact that the

[2]   CEPII (Centre d'Études Prospectives et d'Informations Internationales) is the main French research center in international economics, which produces studies, research, databases and analyses on the world economy. Among its databases is BACI, which provides disaggregated data on bilateral trade flows for more than 5,000 products and 200 countries. The database is built from data directly reported by each country to the UN Statistical Division as inputs to the UN Comtrade.

Figure 2.3: International Merchandise Trade, 2019

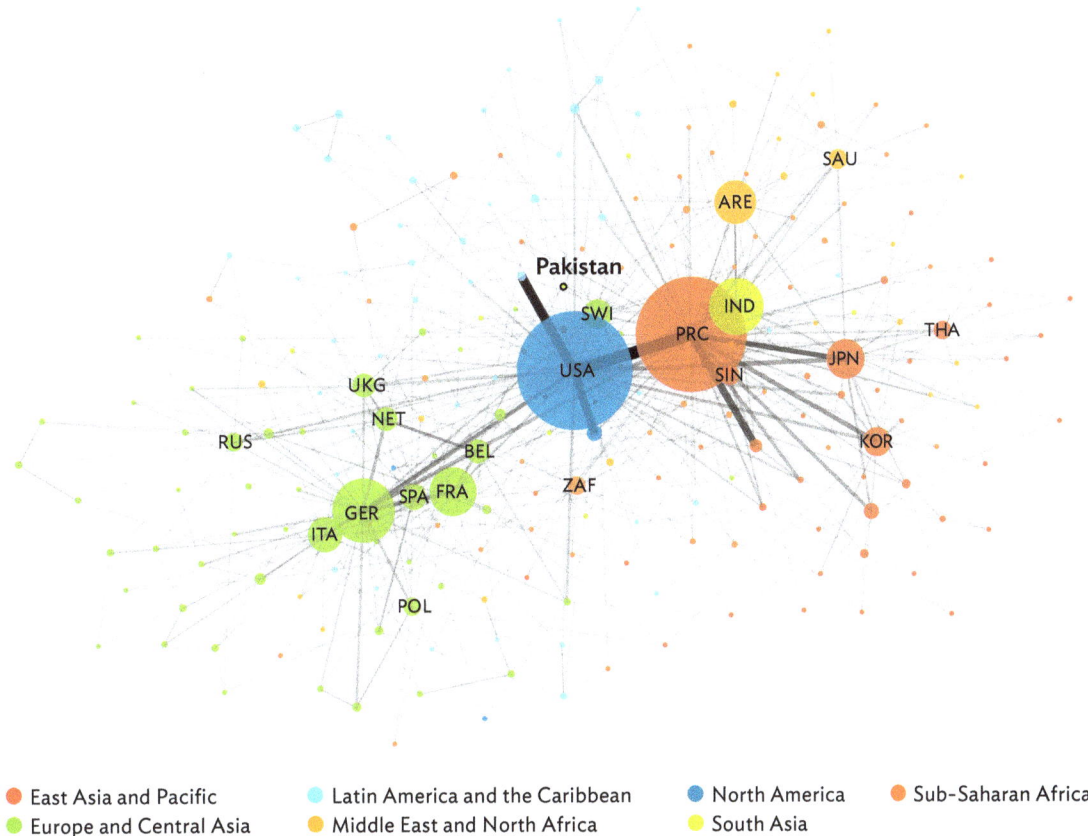

● East Asia and Pacific ○ Latin America and the Caribbean ● North America ● Sub-Saharan Africa
● Europe and Central Asia ● Middle East and North Africa ● South Asia

ARE = United Arab Emirates, BEL = Belgium, FRA = France, GER = Germany, IND = India, ITA = Italy, JPN = Japan, KOR = Republic of Korea, NET = Netherlands, POL = Poland, PRC = People's Republic of China, RUS = Russian Federation, SAU = Saudi Arabia, SIN = Singapore, SPA = Spain, SWI = Switzerland, THA = Thailand, UKG = United Kingdom, USA = United States, ZAF = South Africa.
Notes: Each node represents a country or economy. Nodes appear only if they meet a threshold of connectedness, defined as being among the three largest importers of some node. Node sizes reflect the number of such links connected to the node, while edge thickness reflects the dollar value of the trade flow. Nodes are arranged using the *graphopt* layout algorithm. Regional groupings are from the World Bank. Taipei,China is proxied by "Other Asia, not elsewhere specified."
Source: CEPII. BACI International Trade Database (accessed 1 August 2021).

largest nodes are the United States and the People's Republic of China (PRC) means they appear among the top three importers of other nodes the most. The thickness of a link, meanwhile, is proportional to the value of trade it is representing. Again, the thickest link is that between the United States and the PRC, indicating that it is the most significant bilateral relationship in the world.

Color coding by geographic region reveals a gravity-type clustering of nodes, i.e., countries that are physically near each other on the map tend to trade more with each other. This, however, is belied by Pakistan, whose top trading partners are outside South Asia. The network draws four links connecting to it: outward to its top three importers the United States, Germany, and the PRC; and inward from Afghanistan, for which it is the second-largest importer.

The advantage of the UN Comtrade and/or CEPII BACI data is its granularity, reporting exports of products at the 6-digit level of the Harmonized System (HS). It is possible to establish, therefore, that in 2019, Pakistan's top goods export was "Trousers, bib and brace overalls, breeches and shorts: men's or boys', of cotton (not knitted or crocheted)" (HS code 6203.42), valued at $1.7 billion. Product categories may be aggregated into broader categories, if needed. The "chapter" of 6203.42, for example, is 62, "Articles of apparel and clothing accessories, not knitted or crocheted."

Figure 2.4 examines the product makeup of Pakistan's merchandise exports over 2002–2019 by aggregating HS codes into nine broad groupings. Exports are overwhelmingly dominated by textiles and footwear, which in 2019 accounted for 56% of export value or $15.5 billion. While down from its almost three-fourths share in 2002, it is still far larger than any other grouping. Within textiles and footwear, a few subgroups dominate. "Cotton trousers"—shorthand for all trousers, bib-and-brace overalls, breeches, and shorts made of cotton, whether hand- or machine-sewn—accounted for 11.6% of 2019 export value, almost double its 6.0% share in 2012. This is largely oriented toward the European and North American markets, which took in 90% of such exports in 2019. Other major subgroups include all types of bed linen (8.9% in 2019) and all types of kitchen and toilet linen (3.8% in 2019).

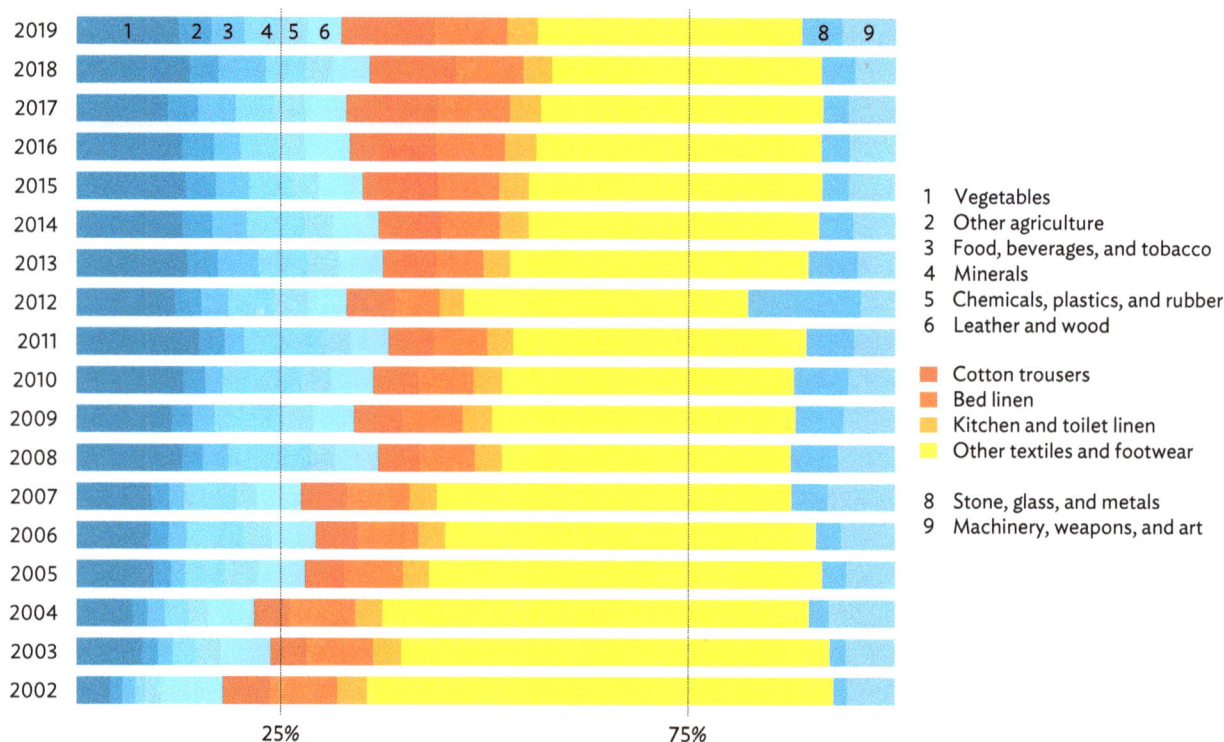

Figure 2.4: Merchandise Exports by Broad Product Groupings, Pakistan, 2002–2019

1 Vegetables
2 Other agriculture
3 Food, beverages, and tobacco
4 Minerals
5 Chemicals, plastics, and rubber
6 Leather and wood

Cotton trousers
Bed linen
Kitchen and toilet linen
Other textiles and footwear

8 Stone, glass, and metals
9 Machinery, weapons, and art

Notes: Broad product groupings are based on the chapters of the Harmonized System, 2002 edition. "Vegetables" covers 06–14. "Other agriculture" covers 01–05 and 15. "Food, beverages and tobacco" covers 16–24. "Minerals" covers 25–27. "Chemicals, plastics and rubber" covers 28–40. "Leather and wood" covers 41–49. "Textiles and footwear" covers 50–67. "Stone, glass and metals" covers 68–83. "Machinery, weapons and art" covers 84–97. Within "Textiles and footwear", "Cotton trousers" (6103.42, 6104.62, 6203.42 and 6204.62), "Bed linen" (6302.10–6302.39), and "Kitchen and toilet linen" (6302.60–6302.99) are separately identified.
Source: CEPII. BACI International Trade Database (accessed 1 August 2021).

Testifying to the persistence of agriculture in Pakistan's economy is the significance of "vegetables" in its exports, whose share of 12.5% was the second-largest in 2019. Dominant under this category is milled rice, sent mostly to the PRC and the Middle East. Other major exports include those under machinery, weapons, and art, particularly medical, surgical, or dental instruments and appliances, most of which go to the United States and Mexico.

The dominance of textile products in Pakistan's exports raises the issue of diversification—or potentially the lack of it. Concentrating too much on only a few sectors or products poses risks to an economy since shocks to the dominant sector can more easily cause an economy-wide recession. However, while textile exports are indeed very significant for Pakistan, it does appear to export several different types of textile products, from apparel to bed sheets to kitchen towels. To properly quantify the overall diversification of Pakistan's exports, the Herfindahl–Hirschman Index (HHI) is computed on the two-digit level of its HS product categories. See Box 2 for more details on this methodology.

Box 2: Measuring Export Diversification

Export diversification refers to the diversity in products exported by an economy. To quantify this, this report uses a widely accepted measure of concentration, the Herfindahl–Hirschman Index (HHI), computed by summing the squared share of each entity in the population in question. Formally,

$$HHI = 100 \times \sum_{i}^{N} s_i^2,$$

where s_i is the share of entity i and N is the number of entities in the population. The HHI ranges from $1/N$ to 100, with higher numbers indicating greater concentration, or conversely, lower diversification. While originally devised to measure market concentration, it is applicable to a wide range of distribution-related contexts.

The HHI is sensitive to N, with the index tending to be lower as N gets bigger. For this report, the two-digit level of the Hamonized System is used, which separately identifies 97 products. This is chosen since lower levels of disaggregation allow for the possibility of exporting many types of the same products, giving a somewhat artificial sense of diversification. For example, an economy exporting sardines, tuna, mackerel, salmon, and halibut would be treated in the present approach as simply concentrating in fish.

Source: W. F. Shughart. 2008. Industrial Concentration. In D. R. Henderson, ed. *Concise Encyclopedia of Economics*. 2nd ed. Indianapolis, IN: Library of Economics and Liberty.

Figure 2.5 plots the exports HHI of Pakistan along with, for comparison, its neighbors Bangladesh, India, and Sri Lanka. As a textiles-oriented trader in Asia and the Pacific, Cambodia is included as well. The measures suggest that Pakistan's exports remain relatively diverse, its HHI going down slightly from 9.1 points to 8.2 points between 2005 and 2019. This is in contrast to two of the most prolific textiles exporters in the world, Bangladesh and Cambodia; although, it must be noted that trends for each are going in opposite directions. Bangladesh has by far the most concentrated exports basket; its HHI leaping from 29.0 points in 2005 to 37.7 points in 2019. While Cambodia began as the most concentrated in the sample, it has since diversified somewhat, achieving an HHI of 17.6 points in 2019, within reach of Sri Lanka's 14.0 points. Pakistan's exports, however, remain less diverse than India's, whose continental size likely helps sustain a wider variety of exports. In 2019, India's HHI was only 5.2 points, down from 6.0 points in 2005.

Figure 2.5: Merchandise Export Diversification, Selected Countries, 2005, 2010, 2015, and 2019

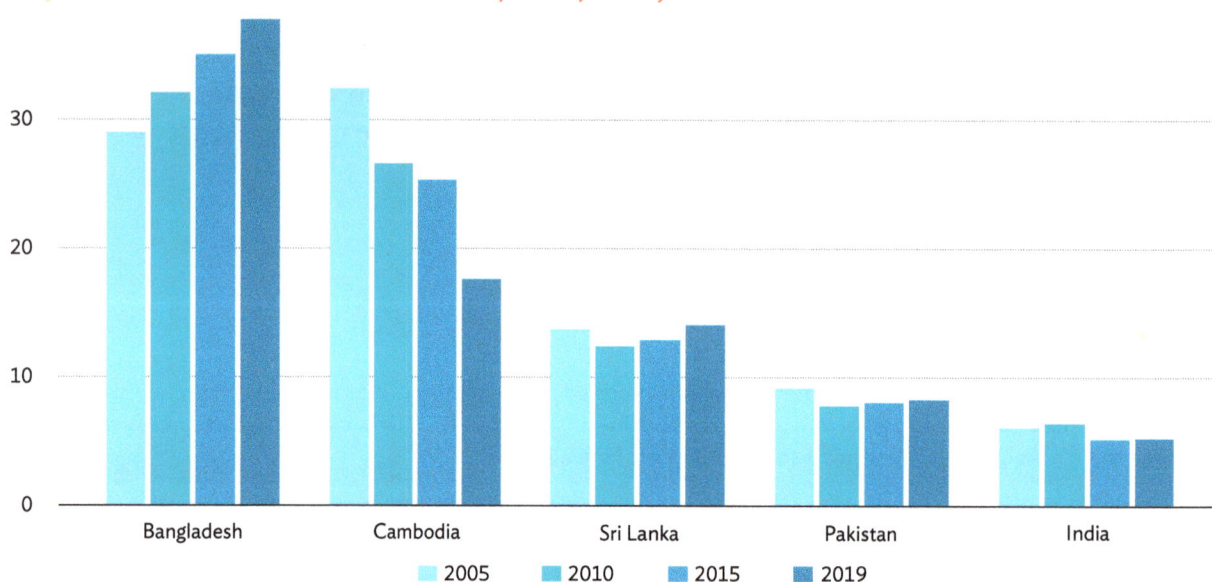

Notes: Diversification is measured by the Herfindahl–Hirschman Index. Products are disaggregated at the two-digit level of the Harmonized System, 2002 edition.
Sources: Asian Development Bank estimates; and CEPII. BACI International Trade Database (accessed 1 August 2021).

In summary, this chapter has shown that Pakistan has historically experienced uneven growth and remains among the least open economies in the world, even after taking its relatively large size into account. What it does export is dominated by textile products and rice, though a formal measure of concentration suggests that its exports basket is on the whole quite diversified, especially compared with other major textile exporters Bangladesh and Cambodia. Its top trading partners are the United States, Europe, and the PRC, though it also sells much of its rice to the Middle East. The only economy for which it is a major market is its northern neighbor Afghanistan.

Chapter 3

PARTICIPATION IN GLOBAL VALUE CHAINS

A global value chain (GVC) is a type of production arrangement where different stages are undertaken in different territories, typically by different firms.[3] GVCs intensified in the 1990s as several trends took shape, including leaps in information and communication technologies, the spread of market economies in the former Communist states, and perhaps most importantly, the opening up of the People's Republic of China (PRC) to world trade. All these encouraged managers to relocate certain stages of production to where they can be performed at the lowest cost.

Among the numerous consequences of GVCs is statistical. Trade is generally reported in gross bilateral terms: country A's exports to country B. GVCs complicate this in two ways. First, some of A's exports may contain value added that did not originate in A. Second, not all of A's exports to B are finally consumed in B. Imported inputs on the one hand and reexports on the other mean that third countries may have an indirect relationship with each other via the bilateral link between A and B, relationships that are hidden in standard trade data.

This chapter explores Pakistan's engagement with GVCs by combining the rich information found in the Multiregional Input–Output (MRIO) database of the Asian Development Bank (ADB) with the GVC-focused input–output models that have been developed in the literature. The ADB MRIO database is available for the years 2000 and 2007–2020 and covers 62 economies, including 26 from ADB's member economies in Asia and the Pacific. More details on this database are given in Box 1.

Accounting for intersector linkages allows this chapter to take a value-added approach to Pakistan's trade. This begins with a careful decomposition of its exports into various value-added categories. Using the methodology in ADB (2021), gross exports are divided into those whose value added originated domestically (DVA), those that originated from foreign sources (FVA), and those that did not originate from value added at all. The last, called pure double-counting (PDC), refers to duplicated recordings of the same value added, crossing the same border more than once. DVA, in turn, is further divided into (i) directly absorbed value-added exports (DAVAX) by the importer, (ii) those reexported by the importer and eventually absorbed abroad (REX), and (iii) those reexported by the importer and eventually return to and are consumed by the exporter ("reflection", or REF). See Box 3 for more details on this framework.

---

[3] For an overview of the concept, see Inomata (2017).

Box 3: Decomposing Exports into Value-Added Categories

The prevalence of cross-border production sharing—what this report calls global value chains (GVCs)—has meant that flows of value added may increasingly diverge from the flows captured in standard trade statistics. Datasets like balance of payments accounts and the United Nations Comtrade database record bilateral flows from one economy to another, but do not typically provide information on the value-added makeup of such flows.

In a framework pioneered by Koopman, Wang, and Wei (2014) and refined by Borin and Mancini (2019), information from an intercountry input–output table is used to decompose export flows into value-added categories. The Asian Development Bank (ADB) (2021) gives an exposition of the particular methodology employed in this report. To summarize, exports are broken down into five main categories, as shown in the figure below.

Decomposition of Home's Exports to Partner

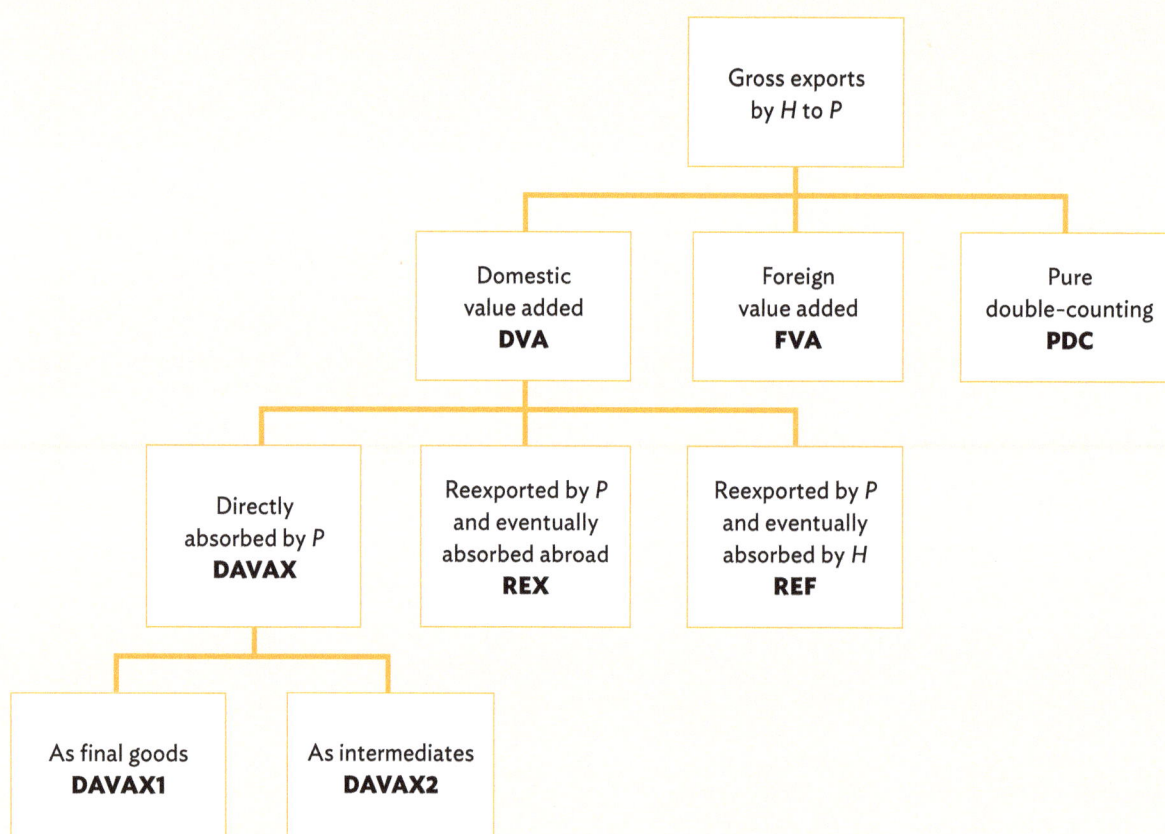

H = home, P = partner
Source: Asian Development Bank. 2021. *Key Indicators for Asia and the Pacific 2021*. Manila.

DAVAX are exports of domestic value added that are directly absorbed by the importer. It will be useful to subdivide this into DAVAX1 and DAVAX2, corresponding to exports of final goods and exports of intermediates, respectively. REX and REF are exports of domestic value added that are reexported by the importer, to eventually be absorbed abroad (REX) or returned to and absorbed by the exporter (REF). FVA are foreign value added embedded in exports, arising from the use of imported inputs. Finally, PDC are the pure double-counting that results from value added crossing the same border more than once. The levels, shares, and trends of each of these categories provide insights into an economy's engagement with GVCs.

continued on next page.

Box 3 *continued.*

A useful statistic derived from this framework is the GVC participation rate. ADB (2021) identifies two approaches to measuring this. The trade-based approach, used among others by Hummels, Ishii, and Yi (2001) and Borin and Mancini (2019), is computed as

$$GVCP^{\text{Trade}} = \frac{REX + REF}{\text{Exports}} + \frac{FVA + PDC}{\text{Exports}}$$

This rate may be divided into a forward participation rate and a backward participation rate, given by the first and second terms, respectively.

The second approach is due to Wang, Wei, Yu, and Zhu (2017). This production-based GVC participation rate is computed as

$$GVCP^{\text{Production}} = \frac{DAVAX2 + REX + REF}{GDP}$$

where GDP is the gross domestic product.

Sources:
Asian Development Bank. 2021. *Key Indicators for Asia and the Pacific 2021*. Manila.
A. Borin and M. Mancini. 2019. Measuring What Matters in Global Value Chains and Value-Added Trade. *Policy Research Working Paper*. No. 8804. Washington, DC: World Bank.
D. Hummels, J. Ishii, and K. M. Yi. 2001. The Nature and Growth of Vertical Specialization in World Trade. *Journal of International Economics*. 54 (1). pp. 75–96.
R. Koopman, Z. Wang, and S. Wei. 2014. Tracing Value-Added and Double Counting in Gross Exports. *American Economic Review*. 104 (2). pp. 459–494.
Z. Wang, S. Wei, X. Yu, and K. Zhu. 2017. Measures of Participation in Global Value Chains and Global Business Cycles. *NBER Working Paper*. No. 23222. Cambridge, MA: National Bureau of Economic Research.

Figure 3.1 presents the decomposition of Pakistan's exports into the five categories described. The largest share is invariably that of DAVAX, also called direct trading. This is the kind of trade one typically imagines when one talks about, say, Pakistan exporting to the United States, in that one conceives of Pakistani value added flowing to the United States to be consumed by Americans. The presence of GVCs may belie this, but DAVAX isolates the portion of gross exports for which this direct type of relationship always applies. In 2020, this amounted to $18.9 billion against gross exports of $24.7 billion.

The remaining portion of exports may then be called indirect trading. For Pakistan, only the REX and FVA categories are significant. REX indicates the continued flow of Pakistani value added down the value chain and is thus a measure of forward integration. FVA indicates the extent of imported inputs embedded in Pakistan's exports and is thus a measure of backward integration. In 2020, REX amounted to $3.3 billion while FVA amounted to $2.4 billion. Total indirect trading, equal to the sum of REX, REF, FVA, and PDC, was $5.8 billion.

Figure 3.1: Decomposition of Exports into Value-Added Categories, Pakistan, 2000, 2007–2020 ($ billion)

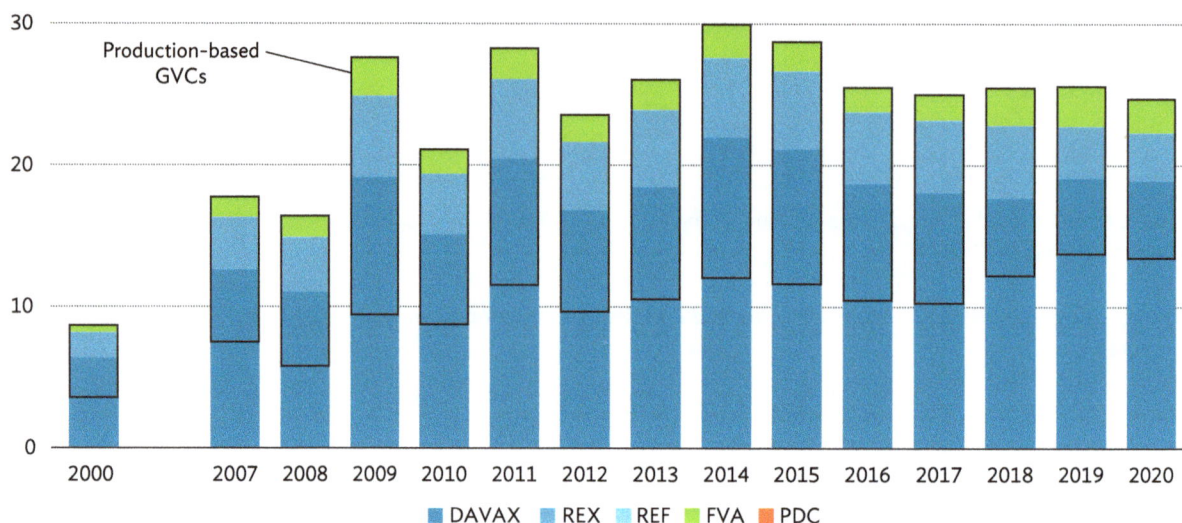

GVC = global value chain.

Notes: Gross exports are decomposed using the methodology in Asian Development Bank (2021). DAVAX are directly absorbed domestic value-added exports. REX are domestic value-added exports reexported by direct importer and eventually absorbed abroad. REF are domestic value-added exports reexported by direct importer and eventually returned to and absorbed at home. FVA are foreign value added embedded in gross exports. PDC are pure double-counting, a result of value added crossing the same border more than once. The boxed portions measure global value chain production according to Wang, Wei, Yu, and Zhu (2017).

Sources: Asian Development Bank (ADB). 2021. *Key Indicators for Asia and the Pacific 2021*. Manila; ADB. Multiregional Input–Output Database (accessed 1 August 2021); ADB estimates; and Z. Wang, S. Wei, X. Yu, and K. Zhu. 2017. Measures of Participation in Global Value Chains and Global Business Cycles. *NBER Working Paper*. No. 23222. Cambridge, MA: National Bureau of Economic Research.

Pakistan's top trading partners differ depending on the value-added category being looked at. It was established in Chapter 2 that the United States, Europe, and the PRC are the top destinations for Pakistan's exports. Though this had only taken merchandise exports into account, Figure 3.2 shows that including services exports changes little: the United States, the PRC, Germany, and the United Kingdom took in some 48.5% of Pakistan's exports in 2020. Moreover, considering that the majority of its trade is of the direct kind, it is no surprise that the ranking hardly changes when looking specifically at DAVAX.

It is the categories under indirect trading where rankings change substantially. For both REX and FVA, the PRC replaces the United States as Pakistan's top trading partner. Some 15.8% of Pakistan's exports that would undergo reexporting made their first landing in the PRC. Bangladesh also gets a more prominent role, receiving 7.8% of exports that would undergo reexporting. On the other hand, some 17.4% of the imported inputs embedded in Pakistan's exports came from the PRC, followed by 12.8% that came from the United States. Interestingly, in none of these categories did Pakistan's sizable neighbor India appear.

Figure 3.2: Top Ten Trading Partners by Value-Added Category, Pakistan, 2020
(%)

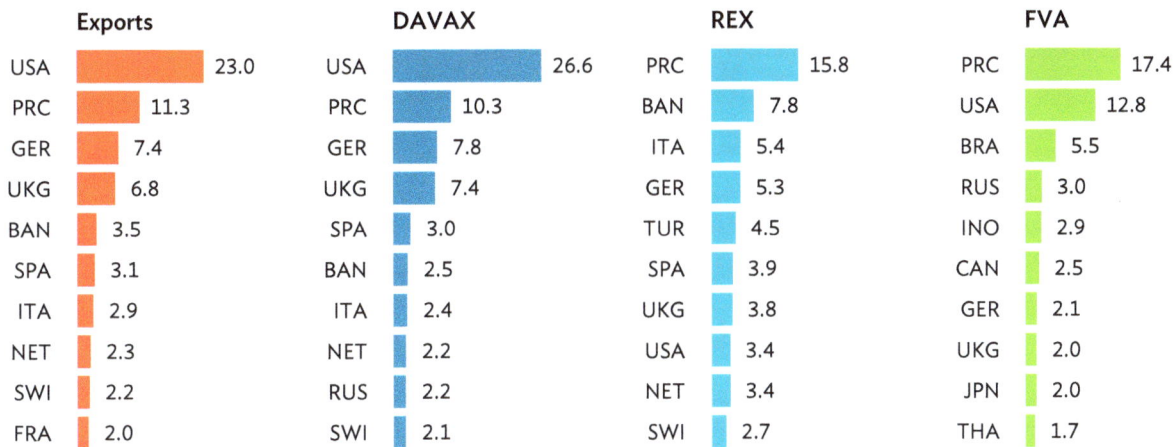

Exports		DAVAX		REX		FVA	
USA	23.0	USA	26.6	PRC	15.8	PRC	17.4
PRC	11.3	PRC	10.3	BAN	7.8	USA	12.8
GER	7.4	GER	7.8	ITA	5.4	BRA	5.5
UKG	6.8	UKG	7.4	GER	5.3	RUS	3.0
BAN	3.5	SPA	3.0	TUR	4.5	INO	2.9
SPA	3.1	BAN	2.5	SPA	3.9	CAN	2.5
ITA	2.9	ITA	2.4	UKG	3.8	GER	2.1
NET	2.3	NET	2.2	USA	3.4	UKG	2.0
SWI	2.2	RUS	2.2	NET	3.4	JPN	2.0
FRA	2.0	SWI	2.1	SWI	2.7	THA	1.7

BAN = Bangladesh, BRA = Brazil, CAN = Canada, FRA = France, GER = Germany, INO = Indonesia, ITA = Italy, JPN = Japan, NET = Netherlands, PRC = People's Republic of China, RUS = Russian Federation, SPA = Spain, SWI = Switzerland, THA = Thailand, TUR = Turkey, UKG = United Kingdom, USA = United States.
Notes: Gross exports are decomposed using the methodology in Asian Development Bank (2021). DAVAX are directly absorbed domestic value-added exports. REX are domestic value-added exports reexported by direct importer and eventually absorbed abroad. FVA are foreign value-added embedded in gross exports.
Sources: Asian Development Bank (ADB). 2021. *Key Indicators for Asia and the Pacific 2021*. Manila; ADB. Multiregional Input–Output Database (accessed 1 August 2021); and ADB estimates.

Quantifying the importance of GVCs in Pakistan's economy is the GVC participation rate. Two approaches are possible: (i) a trade-based approach, which looks at the share of indirect trading in exports; and (ii) a production-based approach, which looks at the share of domestic value added (i.e., GDP) that is exported in an unfinished state. The trade-based approach may further be divided into a forward and a backward participation rate, corresponding to the forward and backward integration into GVCs discussed above. Exports included in the production-based approach, meanwhile, are marked by the boxed regions in Figure 3.1. More details on computing participation rates are provided in Box 3.

Figure 3.3 looks at the historical trend in Pakistan's participation rates, while Figure 3.4 compares these rates with those of related economies. The fact that forward participation is much higher than backward participation in the trade-based approach implies that Pakistan tends to be situated at the more upstream sections of GVCs—i.e., Pakistan's inputs are used by other economies to a greater degree than other economies' inputs are used by Pakistan. Beginning 2017, however, the forward and backward rates began to move closer together, with forward participation rates falling and backward participation rates rising. From a gap of 13.0 percentage points in 2017, just 3.8 points separated the two rates by 2020.

Figure 3.3: Global Value Chain Participation Rates, Pakistan, 2000, 2007–2020 (%)

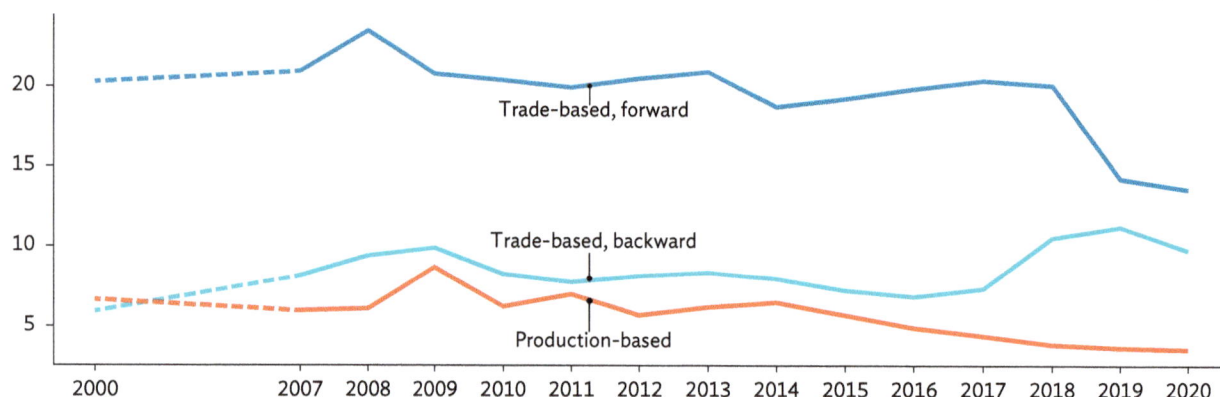

Notes: Participation rates are computed using the methodology in Asian Development Bank (2021). The forward trade-based participation rate is the share of domestic value-added exports reexported by the direct importer in gross exports. The backward trade-based participation rate is the share of foreign value-added and pure double-counting in gross exports. The production-based participation rate is the share of unfinished exports in gross exports.
Sources: Asian Development Bank (ADB). 2021. *Key Indicators for Asia and the Pacific 2021*. Manila; ADB. Multiregional Input–Output Database (accessed 1 August 2021); and ADB estimates.

Overall, GVC participation rates in Pakistan are low, consistent with its equally low trade-to-GDP ratio shown in Figure 2.2. Of the countries sampled in Figure 3.4, Pakistan was at or near the bottom. Indeed, South Asia as a whole (except Maldives) exhibited low participation in GVCs, its members ranking below the world average. While other developing countries, notably Viet Nam and Cambodia, have greatly expanded their GVC engagement since 2000, Pakistan's rates have stayed within a tight range over the course of 2 decades.

Figure 3.4: Global Value Chain Participation Rates, Selected Countries, 2000, 2010, and 2020 (%)

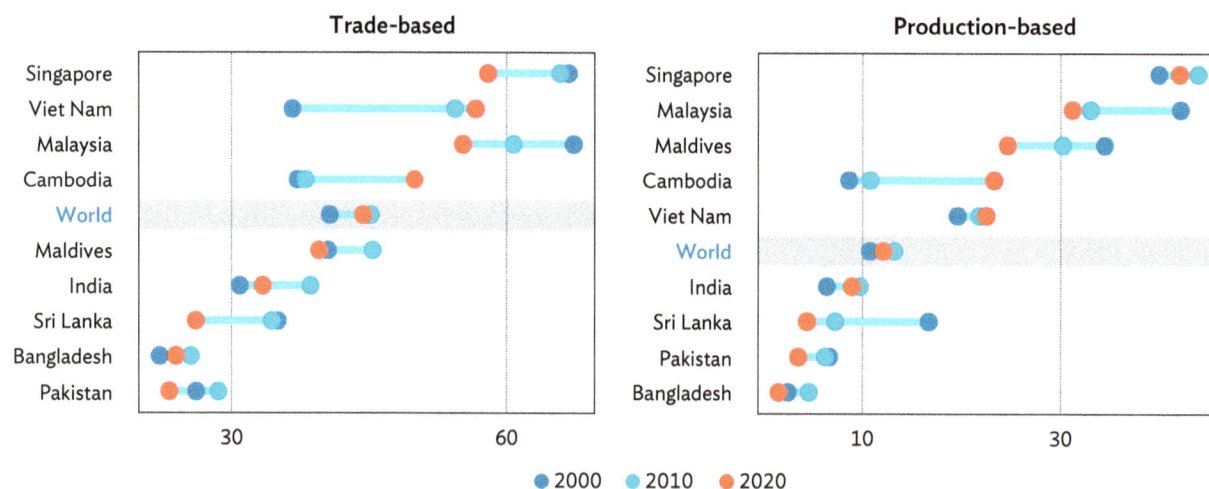

Notes: Participation rates are computed using the methodology in Asian Development Bank (2021). The trade-based participation rate is the share of indirect trade in gross exports. The production-based participation rate is the share of unfinished exports in gross exports.
Sources: Asian Development Bank (ADB). 2021. *Key Indicators for Asia and the Pacific 2021*. Manila; ADB. Multiregional Input–Output Database (accessed 1 August 2021); and ADB estimates.

Aggregate-level rates may mask differences across sectors. Figure 3.5 applies the exports decomposition framework at the sector level, where sectors are identified by the sector that actually exports, rather than the sector from which the value added originated from. Thus, textiles exports, for example, may contain value added from other sectors, but the good that is actually exported is classified under the textiles sector. This approach was chosen to allow for comparability with the aggregate decomposition.

Figure 3.5: Decomposition of Exports into Value-Added Categories by Sector, Pakistan, 2020 (%)

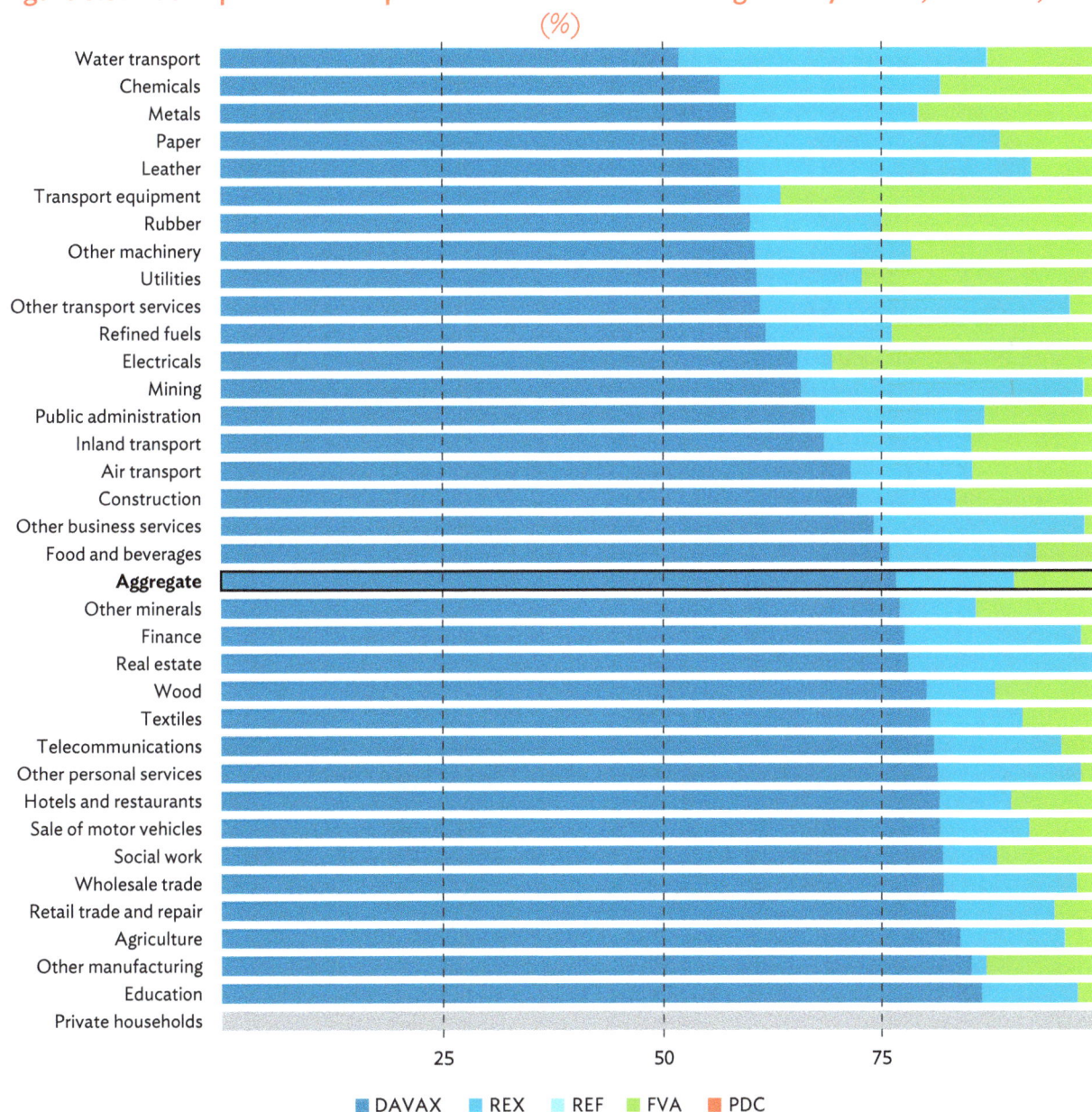

Notes: Gross exports are decomposed using the methodology in Asian Development Bank (2021). DAVAX are directly absorbed domestic value-added exports. REX are domestic value-added exports reexported by direct importer and eventually absorbed abroad. REF are domestic value-added exports reexported by direct importer and eventually returned to and absorbed at home. FVA are foreign value-added embedded in gross exports. PDC are pure double-counting, a result of value-added crossing the same border more than once. Sectors disaggregation is by export sector.
Sources: Asian Development Bank (ADB). 2021. *Key Indicators for Asia and the Pacific 2021*. Manila; ADB. Multiregional Input–Output Database (accessed 1 August 2021); and ADB estimates.

The sector with the highest (trade-based) rate of GVC participation was water transport-related services. With a forward rate of 35.3% and a backward rate of 12.8%, its total participation rate of 48.1% came close to Cambodia's aggregate rate of 50.0% in 2020. However, since actual exports in this sector was a mere $152 million (against total exports of $24.7 billion), its GVC activities may not amount to much. More consequential was the metals sector, which had both a high participation rate (41.6%) and a substantial level of exports ($1.1 billion).

As established in Chapter 2, textiles dominate Pakistan's exports. At $14.2 billion, it accounted for 57.2% of total exports in 2020. Much of this stemmed from direct trading, with only 10.6% of its value getting reexported and 8.8% of its value originating from foreign value added—for a total participation rate of 19.4%. A large fraction of the trading was not integrated into GVCs. However, because of its overall size, absolute GVC exports were relatively substantial. Reexported value amounted to $3.3 billion, while foreign value added amounted to $2.4 billion, both of which dwarfed total exports in the metals sector. Thus, despite its low participation rate, textiles remain the most important sector in terms of Pakistan's GVC activity.

Another way to characterize GVCs is to measure their lengths. Distance in production can be measured if one adopts the simplification of treating value chains like actual "chains"—i.e., as a sequence of stages that progresses in one direction from beginning to end. Any given firm, therefore, may be positioned in its value chain by measuring, on the one hand, the number of stages separating its output from final consumers (forward production length), and on the other, the number of stages separating its output from primary inputs (backward production length). Averaging these lengths for all the firms in a sector or economy gives the average production lengths. Furthermore, isolating the GVC component of a firm's production results in GVC production lengths. Box 4 provides more details.

Box 4: Measuring Average Production Lengths

While production can take many forms, it is useful to conceive of it as a series of sequential stages, where each stage adds value until a finished product results at the very end. This simplification allows for the calculation of a firm's production length, computed from two perspectives. The forward production length counts the number of stages separating the firm's output from the final consumer. The backward production length counts the number of stages separating its output from primary inputs. Averaging these lengths for all the firms in a sector or economy gives the average production lengths.

Antràs and Chor (2013) propose a methodology for computing average production lengths using information in an input–output table. They first identify the share of an entity's output produced after every possible number of stages. They then use these to take a weighted average of the integers 1, 2, 3, 4, and so on. The result provides the number of stages the bulk of the entity's production concentrates on.

Wang, Wei, Yu, and Zhu (2017b) refine this by defining average lengths for both forward and backward perspectives. Not only can adding them give the total length of a particular value chain, taking their ratio also gives the relative position of the entity in that chain, whether it is relatively more upstream (longer forward length compared with

continued on next page.

Box 4 *continued*.

backward length) or more downstream. Moreover, they apply the decomposition of production in Wang, Wei, Yu, and Zhu (2017a) to isolate the global value chain (GVC) activity of the entity, defined according to the production-based approach (see Box 3).

The resulting GVC production lengths may be divided into two segments: the number of stages that occur within the domestic economy of the exporter and the number of stages that occur abroad.

When computing lengths at the sector level, the methodology of Wang et al. (2017b) identifies sectors by the origin of value added.

Sources:
P. Antràs and D. Chor. 2013. Organizing the Global Value Chain. *Econometrica*. 81 (6). pp. 2127–2204.
Z. Wang, S. Wei, X. Yu, and K. Zhu. 2017a. Measures of Participation in Global Value Chains and Global Business Cycles. *NBER Working Paper*. No. 23222. Cambridge, MA: National Bureau of Economic Research.
Z. Wang, S. Wei, X. Yu, and K. Zhu. 2017b. Characterizing Global Value Chains: Production Length and Upstreamness. N*BER Working Paper*. No. 23261. Cambridge, MA: National Bureau of Economic Research.

Longer production lengths, by involving more rounds of value-added contribution, are associated with more complex value chains (Escaith and Inomata 2013). Thus, it complements the essentially binary approach of the GVC participation rate, which classifies each dollar of exports as either belonging to GVCs or not. In Figure 3.6, GVC lengths in Pakistan at both the aggregate and the sector level for the years 2000, 2010, and 2020 are plotted, specifically highlighting changes between 2000 and 2010 and between 2010 and 2020. Note that, in contrast to Figure 3.5, sectors in Figure 3.6 are identified by the sector from which the value added originated from, following the Wang et al. (2017b) methodology.

At the aggregate, total GVC length was 7.58 stages in 2000, rising to 8.03 in 2010, then rising more modestly to 8.18 by 2020. Across sectors, the general conclusion is that lengths increased between 2000 and 2010 but decreased between 2010 and 2020. The textiles, mining, and other business services sectors exemplify these trends. For mining, while lengths rose substantially from 8.33 stages in 2000 to 9.14 in 2010, they fell back down to 8.81 by 2020. Likewise, for other business services, where GVC lengths went from 7.37 stages in 2000 to 8.50 in 2010 before plunging to 8.08 in 2020.

GVC lengths in the textiles sector had more muted movements, going from 7.00 stages in 2000 to 7.49 in 2010 before easing back to 7.45 by 2020. Bucking the trend is a sector like agriculture, whose GVC lengths had continuously increased throughout the period covered, jumping from 7.63 stages in 2000 to 8.18 in 2010 before jumping again to 8.42 by 2020. Its production-based GVC exports, moreover, are the largest in absolute terms—$2.8 billion in 2020, against a total of $11.3 billion.

Figure 3.6: Global Value Chain Production Lengths by Sector, Pakistan, 2000, 2010, and 2020

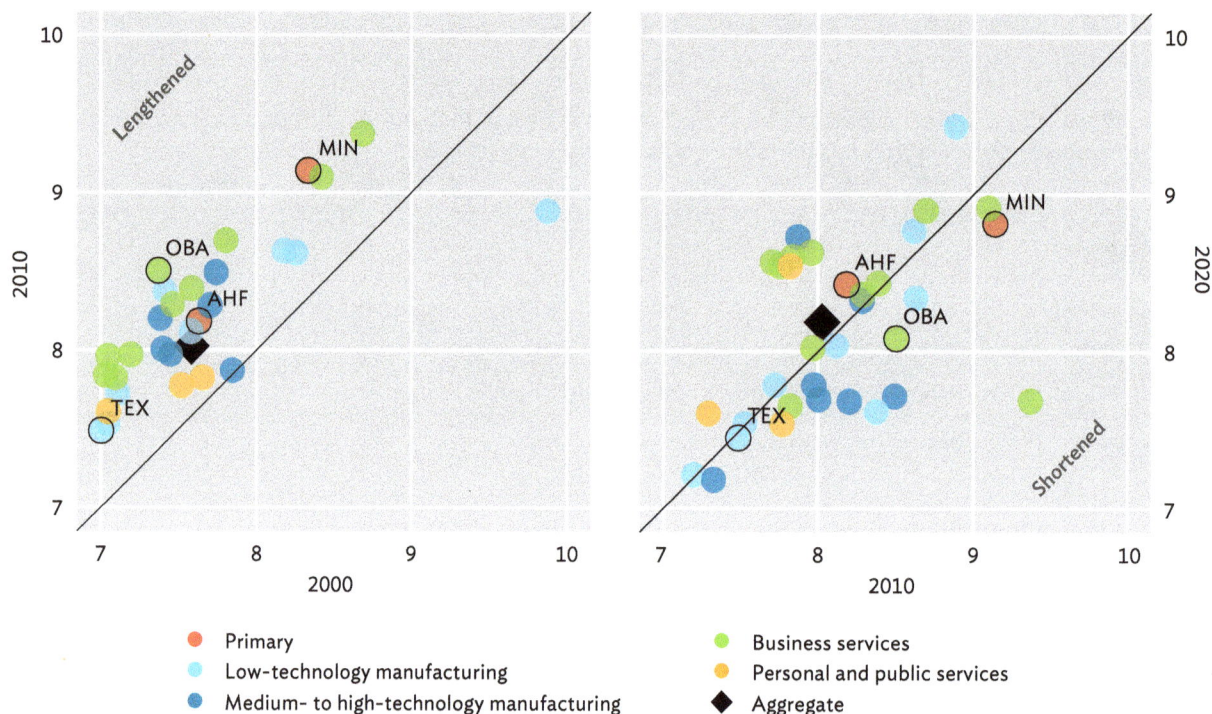

AHF = agriculture, hunting, forestry and fishing; GVC = global value chain; MIN = mining and quarrying; OBA = renting of machinery & equipment and other business activities; TEX = textiles and textile products.
Notes: Average global value chain production lengths are computed using the methodology of Wang, Wei, Yu, and Zhu (2017). Values are the sum of forward and backward production lengths. Sectors with no global value chain production have no lengths and are not included in the chart. Sectors are disaggregated by value-added origins.
Sources: Asian Development Bank (ADB). Multiregional Input–Output Database (accessed 1 August 2021); ADB estimates; and Z. Wang, S. Wei, X. Yu, and K. Zhu. 2017. Characterizing Global Value Chains: Production Length and Upstreamness. *NBER Working Paper*. No. 23261. Cambridge, MA: National Bureau of Economic Research.

Figure 3.7 takes a closer look at the forward GVC length by breaking it down into two segments: stages that occur within the domestic economy and stages that occur abroad. The patterns for textiles show that much of its GVC processing occurs abroad, whereas those in agriculture have both long domestic and foreign segments. This suggests that Pakistan exports relatively simple types of textile products, relying on foreign processing—about 2.09 stages in 2020—to produce the finished goods that reach consumers. Exports of agricultural products, meanwhile, undergo both domestic (2.26 stages in 2020) and foreign processing (2.09 stages in 2020).

The year 2019 is separately identified to reveal, if any, the impact of the 2020 pandemic on GVC lengths. Interestingly, for the four sectors covered, the foreign stages of GVCs invariably lengthened. For textiles in particular, the decline in foreign lengths between 2010 and 2019 was more than made up by the increase in 2020. This points to the resilience of GVCs, at least for Pakistan, though it must be noted that much of the underlying 2020 data in the ADB MRIO database are preliminary. This lengthening will have to be verified as more statistics are finalized in the years to come.

Figure 3.7: Forward Global Value Chain Lengths for Selected Sectors, Pakistan, 2000, 2010, 2019, and 2020

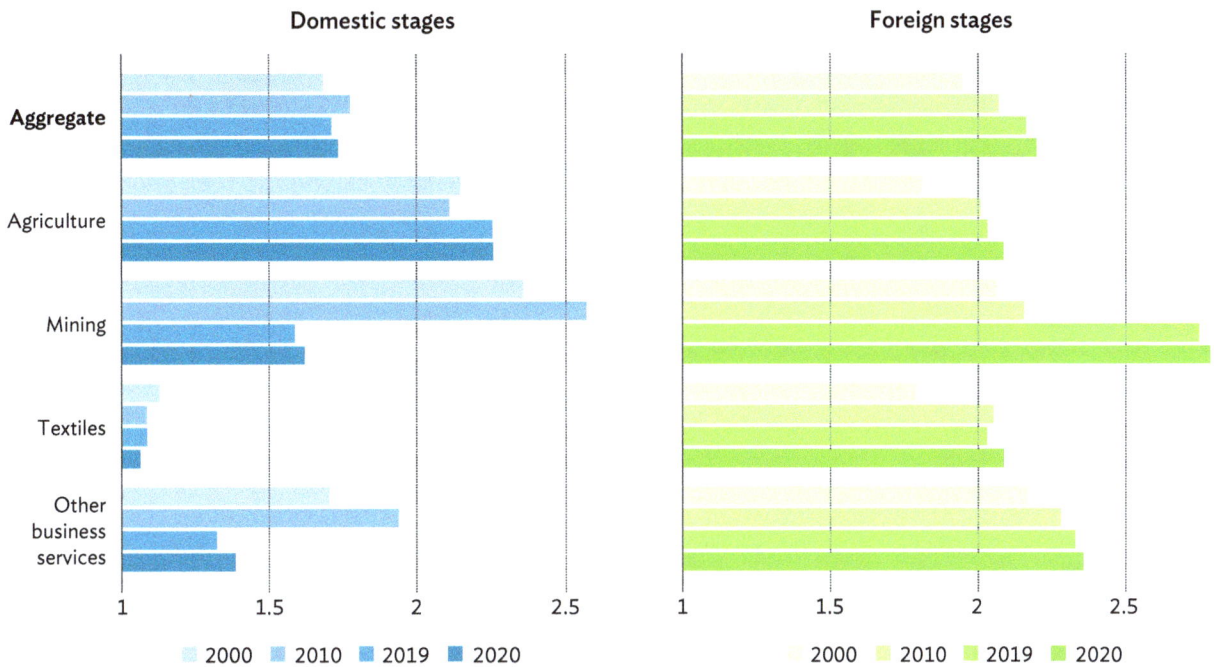

Notes: Average global value chain production lengths are computed using the methodology of Wang, Wei, Yu, and Zhu (2017). Sectors are disaggregated by value-added origins.
Sources: Asian Development Bank (ADB). Multiregional Input–Output Database (accessed 1 August 2021); ADB estimates; and Z. Wang, S. Wei, X. Yu, and K. Zhu. 2017. Characterizing Global Value Chains: Production Length and Upstreamness. *NBER Working Paper*. No. 23261. Cambridge, MA: National Bureau of Economic Research.

In conclusion, this survey into Pakistan's GVC activities points to an economy with relatively low GVC participation. Much of its trade is of the direct kind, where value added solely from Pakistan is sent to and consumed solely by its direct importers. Where it does engage in GVCs, activities concentrate in metals and textiles when looked at by exporting sectors, and agriculture and textiles when looked at by value-added origins. The agriculture sector registers among the longest GVC production lengths, undergoing stages of processing both in Pakistan and abroad. Textiles, on the other hand, are not only shorter overall but rely on much of its processing abroad.

Chapter 4
SPECIALIZATION AND COMPETITIVENESS

This chapter uses global value chain (GVC)-adjusted versions of two classic trade indicators to explore Pakistan's specialization and competitiveness. First, the revealed comparative advantage index, proposed by Balassa (1965), describes patterns of specialization given a country's trade flows. Second, the real effective exchange rate, developed by the International Monetary Fund (Bayoumi, Lee, and Jayanthi 2005), summarizes changes in the price levels of a country's exports relative to its competitors, thereby measuring price competitiveness. Using the frameworks discussed in Chapter 3, both these indicators may be adjusted to reflect value-added rather than gross flows, lending them new relevance in the GVC era.

The concept of comparative advantage originates with the English economist David Ricardo in the 19th century. Balassa operationalized it with his revealed comparative advantage (RCA) index, a ratio that compares the share of a sector in a given country's exports to the average share of that sector across all countries. By convention, an RCA index of greater than 1 indicates a comparative advantage in that sector. This chapter uses two versions of the RCA index to examine Pakistan's sectoral specialization: (i) the standard RCA that uses gross exports, and (ii) a GVC-adjusted RCA that uses value-added exports. Details of this methodology are in Box 5.

Box 5: Calculating the Revealed Comparative Advantage Index

Comparative advantage is used to explain prevailing patterns of trade; the theory is that countries export goods and services they have a comparative advantage in and import the rest. If there are two goods, cars and shirts, and two countries, A and B, and if A's proficiency in making cars relative to shirts is better than B's proficiency in making cars relative to shirts, then A will be exporting cars to B and B will be exporting shirts to A. Note that B might be absolutely better than A at making both cars and shirts: what is crucial is *comparative* proficiency.

Balassa (1965) operationalizes this concept with a ratio called the revealed comparative advantage (RCA) index. Take the share of sector i in a given country's exports and compare it with the average share of sector i across all countries' exports. If it is higher, then the country's export makeup "reveals" it to have a comparative advantage in sector i. If it is lower, then it reveals the absence of a comparative advantage in that sector. Formally, the RCA index of country s for sector i is given by

$$RCA_{(s,i)} = \frac{Exports_{(s,i)}/Exports_s}{\sum_r Exports_{(r,i)}/Exports_r}$$

where the denominator sums across all economies in the world. An RCA index of higher than 1 indicates a comparative advantage in that sector, while an index lower than 1 indicates the lack of a comparative advantage.

continued on next page.

Box 5 *continued.*

As discussed in Asian Development Bank (2021), the RCA index may be adjusted to account for global value chains by using value-added exports. This removes foreign value added and pure double-counting from the country's exports, resulting in an RCA index that is based on domestic value-added flows that are absorbed abroad (see Box 3). In this chapter, sector disaggregations are by value-added origins.

Sources:
Asian Development Bank. 2021. *Key Indicators for Asia and the Pacific 2021*. Manila.
B. Balassa. 1965. Trade Liberalisation and "Revealed" Comparative Advantage. *The Manchester School*. 33 (2). pp. 99–123.

Figure 4.1 charts both RCA indexes for Pakistan across sectors in 2020, ranking them from highest to lowest and tracing how these rankings change as the standard index is adjusted for GVCs. Some similarities emerge. Consistent with previous chapters, textiles had by far the highest RCA index in either formulation. Using gross exports, textiles had an index of 16.7, meaning its share in Pakistan's exports was 16.7 times larger than its average share across the world in 2020. Removing foreign value added and pure double-counting reduces this to a still-high 10.2. A related sector that Pakistan appears to also be specializing in is leather, which had a gross export index of 2.9 and a value-added export index of 2.4.

Emphasizing Pakistan's concentration in textile and leather goods were its low RCA indexes in all other manufacturing sectors. Electricals, a staple of fast-growing GVC-oriented economies like Viet Nam, registered a gross export index of 1/12 and a value-added export index of 1/13, implying its share in Pakistan's exports was less than a tenth of the world average. The same was observed for metals, transport equipment, and chemicals; particularly acute was "other machinery", which notched just 1/45 for both indexes.

Significant differences are observed for two sectors when comparing the gross with the value-added index: retail trade and agriculture. Both of these had indexes of less than 1 when looking at gross exports, but among the highest indexes when looking at value-added exports. Retail trade may be explained by the fact that services are still not as easily tradable as goods. For Pakistan to record exports in this sector under standard trade statistics, the buyer has to be relatively nearby, like a tourist or a business traveler. Thus, its RCA was an abysmal 1/10,000. However, looking at value-added flows completely changes the picture as the services embedded in exported goods is accounted for. The GVC-adjusted RCA jumps to 2.2, implying that, in value-added terms, Pakistan was specializing in the exports of retail trade services in 2020.

Figure 4.1: Revealed Comparative Advantage Indexes, Pakistan, 2020

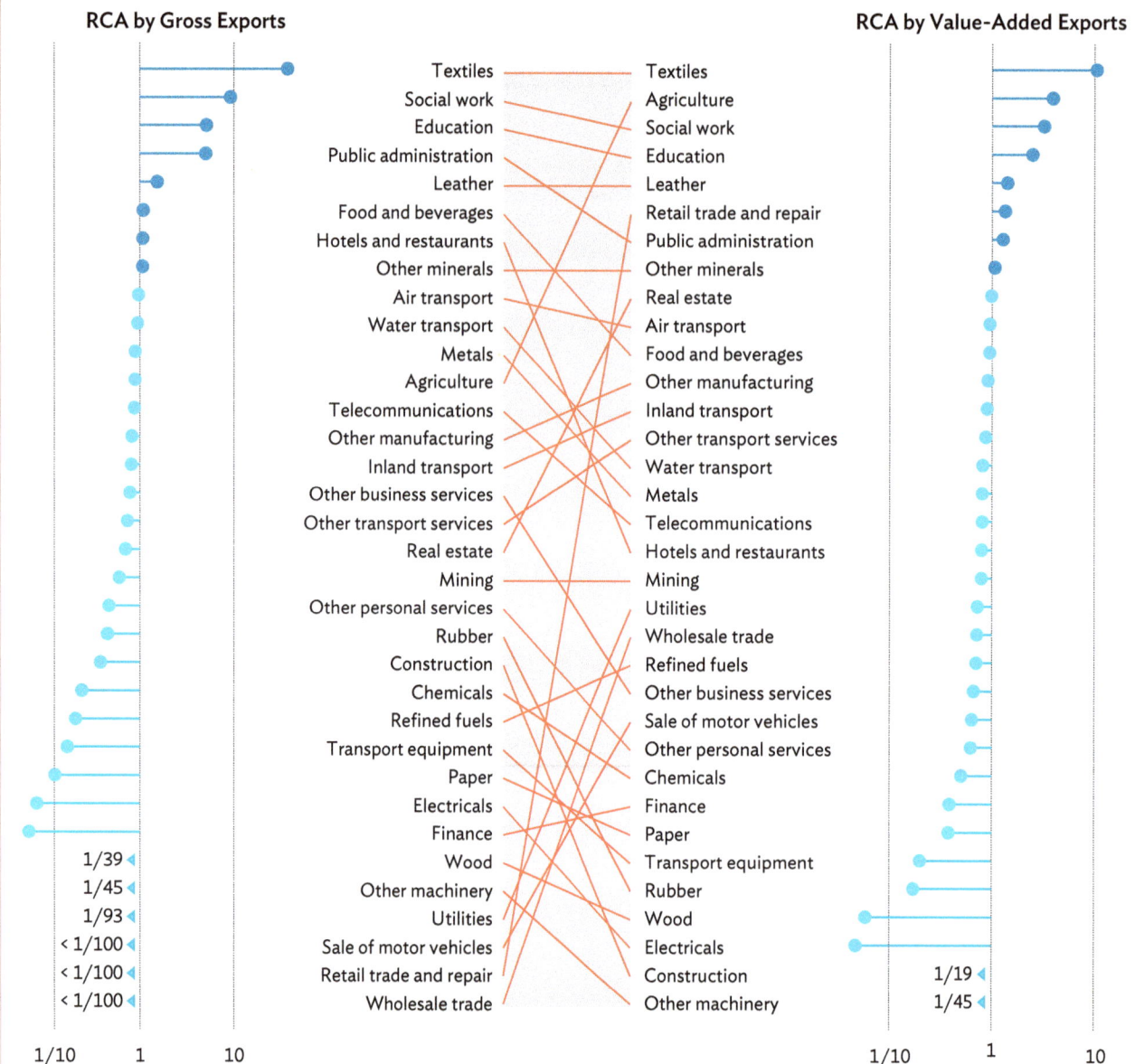

RCA = revealed comparative advantage.
Notes: RCA indexes are computed according to Balassa (1965) and the Asian Development Bank (2021). Sectors with RCA indexes of greater than 1 are sectors where Pakistan is said to have a revealed comparative advantage in. Value-added exports are exports of domestic value added that are absorbed abroad and disaggregated by origin sectors, computed following ADB (2021). Sectors with no value-added exports are omitted.
Sources: Asian Development Bank (ADB). 2021. *Key Indicators for Asia and the Pacific 2021*. Manila; ADB. Multiregional Input–Output Database (accessed 1 August 2021); ADB estimates; and B. Balassa. 1965. Trade Liberalisation and "Revealed" Comparative Advantage. *The Manchester School*. 33 (2). pp. 99–123.

A similar explanation may be behind the shift in agriculture, in that much of its exports were embedded in goods from other sectors. In particular, while the RCA of agriculture goes up when GVC-adjusted (from 0.6 to 6.4), that of food and beverages goes down (from 1.4 to 0.8), suggesting that exports of food and beverages were mostly composed of value added from the agriculture sector.

In value-added terms, Figure 4.1 shows that Pakistan is an economy that specializes in textiles and agriculture. A question arises, however, on where along these value chains Pakistan is finding its niche. Is it in the upstream sections (closer to primary producers), the downstream sections (closer to final consumers), or somewhere in the middle? To answer this, the forward and backward GVC production lengths of Wang, Wei, Yu, and Zhu (2017b) (described in Box 4) is compared with one another. If the forward length is longer, then the economy is said to be more upstream, while if the backward length is longer, the economy is more downstream.

Using this convention, Figure 4.2 traces Pakistan's position in the textiles and agriculture value chains from 2010 to 2020. For reference, the figure also includes other countries that were found to be specializing in these sectors: Bangladesh, Cambodia, Sri Lanka, and Turkey in textiles; and Brazil, Cambodia, the Lao People's Democratic Republic, and Nepal for agriculture. Dots above the 45-degree line are upstream countries, while dots below the 45-degree line are downstream countries.

Figure 4.2: Positioning in the Textile and Agriculture Global Value Chains, Selected Countries, 2010 and 2020

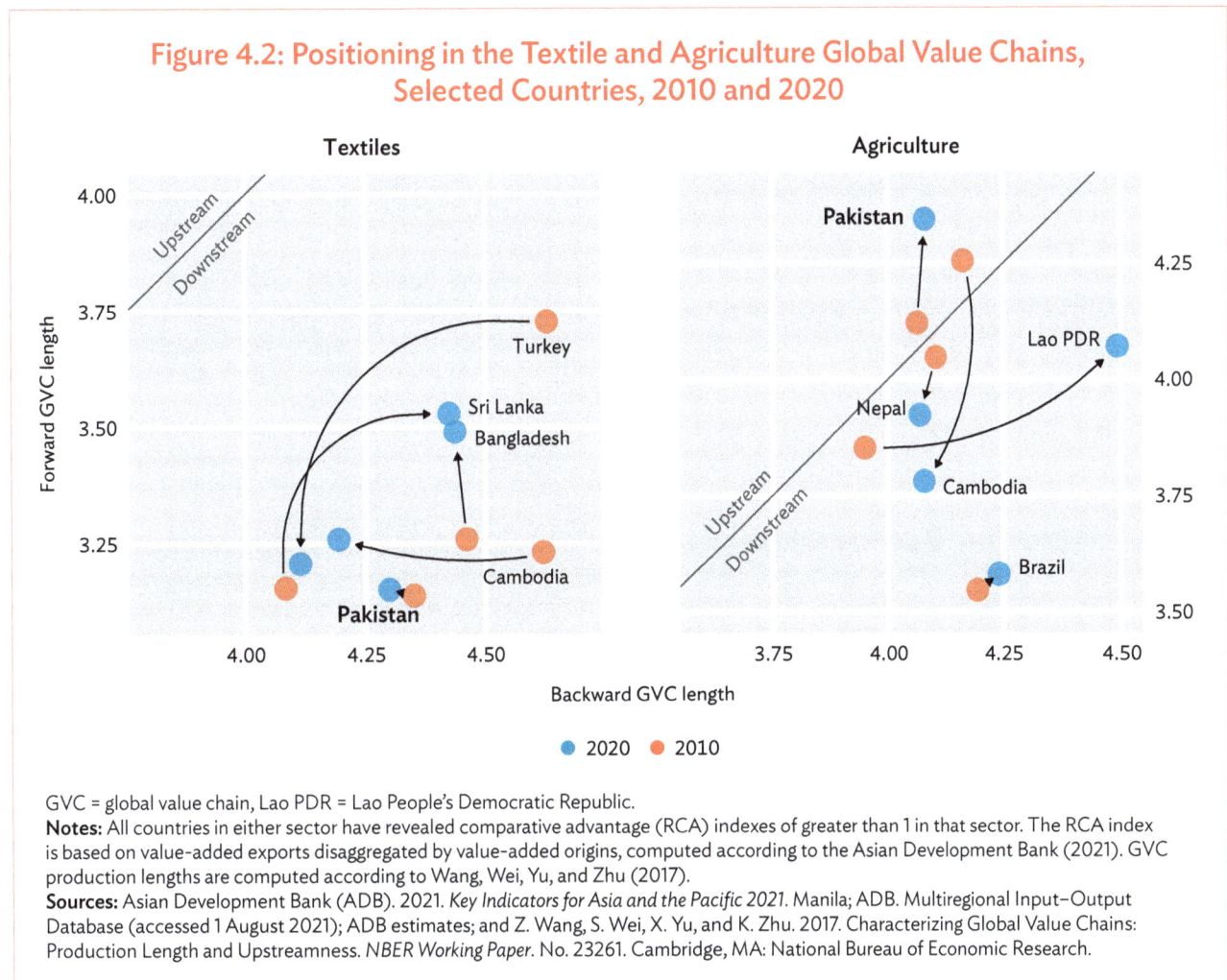

GVC = global value chain, Lao PDR = Lao People's Democratic Republic.
Notes: All countries in either sector have revealed comparative advantage (RCA) indexes of greater than 1 in that sector. The RCA index is based on value-added exports disaggregated by value-added origins, computed according to the Asian Development Bank (2021). GVC production lengths are computed according to Wang, Wei, Yu, and Zhu (2017).
Sources: Asian Development Bank (ADB). 2021. *Key Indicators for Asia and the Pacific 2021*. Manila; ADB. Multiregional Input–Output Database (accessed 1 August 2021); ADB estimates; and Z. Wang, S. Wei, X. Yu, and K. Zhu. 2017. Characterizing Global Value Chains: Production Length and Upstreamness. *NBER Working Paper*. No. 23261. Cambridge, MA: National Bureau of Economic Research.

All five countries specializing in textiles were in the downstream end, suggesting that these countries tended to use designs from abroad to produce textile products that, with little further processing, went straight to final consumers. Pakistan's position did not change much between 2010 and 2020, unlike the more dramatic movements of the other players. Looking only at the blue dots, Pakistan is found to have had the shortest forward GVC length, placing it closest to final consumers, while its backward GVC length was the median of the group.

In contrast, Pakistan was the only country in the upstream region in the agriculture value chain. Between 2010 and 2020, its GVC length from both perspectives increased, though as its forward length increased by much more, its overall position moved further upstream. All other countries were in the downstream end, with Cambodia shifting from upstream to downstream between 2010 and 2020. These suggest that Pakistan is an agriculture exporter whose products undergo plenty of further processing abroad before final consumption. Note, however, that its fairly high backward GVC length means it does also rely on some upstream processing.

Having established the position of Pakistan in the value chains of these two sectors, this chapter turns next to how its price competitiveness has changed over the decade 2010–2019. This is measured by the real effective exchange rate (REER) index. The REER is a price index in the spirit of the GDP deflator and the consumer price index, though it accounts not just for a country's domestic prices but also the prices of its international trade competitors, weighted by the degree to which it competes with them. If the REER goes up, then the country's prices have gone up relative to its competitors; thus, it is said to have lost competitiveness. Likewise, if the REER goes down, then it has gained competitiveness. Moreover, like the RCA index, this chapter implements a refinement of the REER that considers value-added rather than gross flows. Box 6 provides a detailed explanation on the calculation of REER index.

Box 6: Calculating the Real Effective Exchange Rate Index

The real effective exchange rate (REER) is a price index that summarizes a country's prices relative to its trade competitors. Changes in the REER can be thought of as the residual price change after inflation rates and nominal exchange rate movements have been taken into account. Changes in the REER would always be zero under purchasing power parity (PPP), but it generally is not due to factors like home bias, market frictions, and policy (Itskhoki 2020). Because of this, the REER acts like an inverse competitiveness index. Depreciation, which by convention means a fall in the REER, implies that the home country's goods have become relatively cheaper in the markets it competes in and can therefore expect higher demand; appreciation, conversely, is associated with lower demand.

The REER index is a weighted average of bilateral real exchange rates (Chinn 2006). Price levels in countries with whom the home country has more trade have a larger influence in its REER. Formally, the weight country s assigns to the prices of country r is

$$W_{sr} \propto \sum_{u} \left(\frac{p_s Exports_{su}}{p_s Exports_s} \right) \left(\frac{p_r Exports_{ru}}{p_s Demand_u} \right)$$

That is, it is proportional to two fractions summed across all markets u. The first is the importance of market u in s's exports and the second is the market share of r in market u. The higher either of these are, the higher the weight.

continued on next page.

Box 6 *continued.*

The REER itself is obtained by multiplying the weights matrix **W** with the vector of price changes $\hat{p}$:

$$\mathbf{REER} = \mathbf{W} \cdot \hat{\mathbf{p}}$$

Calculating the weights matrix typically relies on trade statistics that only report gross exports, resulting in the implicit assumption that all trade is in final goods (see Box 3). This has grown increasingly untenable with the rise of global value chains (GVCs) (Bems and Johnson 2017). To illustrate, consider a trading relationship where Japan exports electronic components to the People's Republic of China (PRC), who assembles them into toys that then compete with toys from the United States. Suppose there is no direct trade between Japan and the United States. Then in computations of the United States REER, a depreciation of the yen registers no impact, though by decreasing PRC input costs, it may well result in cheaper PRC exports, making United States exports less competitive. In short, if the presence of GVCs is not taken into account, the resulting REER index may miss a lot of relevant nuances.

This chapter implements the GVC-adjusted REERs of Patel, Wang, and Wei (2019). Expanding on Bems and Johnson (2017), they build a dynamic stochastic general equilibrium model using Armington (1969) demand functions to derive a weights matrix at the country-sector level, which may be aggregated to the country level through value-added-weighted averages. This chapter simplifies their model by assuming constant and uniform elasticities.

Sources:
P. S. Armington. 1969. A Theory of Demand for Products Distinguished by Place of Production. *International Monetary Fund Staff Papers.* 16 (1). pp. 159–178.
T. Bayoumi, J. Lee, and S. Jayanthi. 2005. New Rates from New Weights. *IMF Working Paper.* No. WP/05/99. Washington, DC: International Monetary Fund.
R. Bems and R. C. Johnson. 2017. Demand for Value Added and Value-Added Exchange Rates. *American Economic Journal: Macroeconomics.* 9 (4). pp. 45–90.
M. D. Chinn. 2006. A Primer on Real Effective Exchange Rates: Determinants, Overvaluation, Trade Flows and Competitive Devaluation. *Open Economies Review.* 51 (1). pp. 115–143.
O. Itskhoki. 2020. The Story of the Real Exchange Rate. *NBER Working Paper.* No. 28225. Cambridge, MA: National Bureau of Economic Research.
S. Patel, Z. Wang, and S. Wei. 2019. Global Value Chains and Effective Exchange Rates at the Country-Sector Level. *Journal of Money, Credit and Banking.* 51 (1). pp. 7–42.

The two panels of Figure 4.3 show the countries whose prices have the largest weights in Pakistan's textiles and agriculture REERs. These weights reflect the market leaders in the markets Pakistan competes in. For textiles in panel (a), the United States held the single largest weight across 2010–2020. It was established in Chapter 2 that the United States was among the top destinations for Pakistan's textile exports; from this, it can be inferred that the United States itself is the leader in its own market for textiles. Thus, its prices have a large effect on Pakistani competitiveness. Other countries with substantial weight include the PRC and Germany, both of which are also top export destinations.

Figure 4.3: Real Effective Exchange Rate Weights, Selected Sectors, Pakistan, 2010–2020 (%)

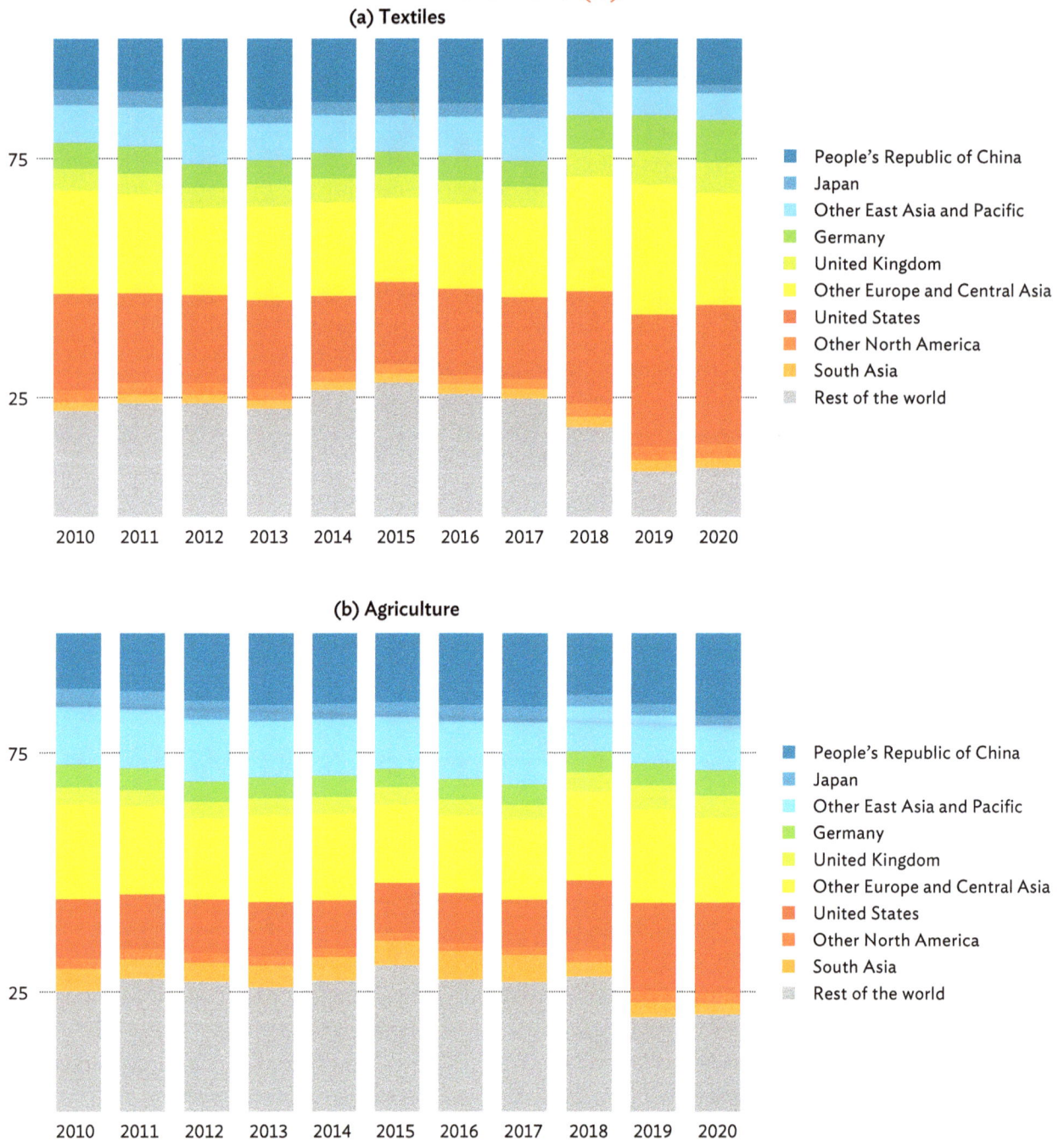

(a) Textiles

Legend:
- People's Republic of China
- Japan
- Other East Asia and Pacific
- Germany
- United Kingdom
- Other Europe and Central Asia
- United States
- Other North America
- South Asia
- Rest of the world

(b) Agriculture

Legend:
- People's Republic of China
- Japan
- Other East Asia and Pacific
- Germany
- United Kingdom
- Other Europe and Central Asia
- United States
- Other North America
- South Asia
- Rest of the world

Note: Weights reflect the importance of each country's prices to Pakistan's sector-level real effective exchange rate index, computed according to Patel, Wang, and Wei (2019).
Sources: Asian Development Bank (ADB). Multiregional Input–Output Database (accessed 1 August 2021); ADB estimates; and S. Patel, Z. Wang, and S. Wei. 2019. Global Value Chains and Effective Exchange Rates at the Country-Sector Level. *Journal of Money, Credit and Banking*. 51 (1). pp. 7–42.

Region-wise, Europe and Central Asia held the largest weight at 38.6%. The fact that the weights of Pakistan's neighbors in South Asia were minuscule suggests that these countries do not have a substantial presence in the markets Pakistan competes in.

Turning to agriculture, panel (b) shows that the same countries are highlighted though their weights differ. The United States and the PRC alternate in holding the largest weight. The share of the residual "rest of the world" is noticeably higher, likely because, as mentioned in Chapter 2, the Middle East is a significant market for Pakistan's rice. The countries of this region are not separately identified in the ADB Multiregional Input–Output (MRIO) database.

Using these weights to take an average of Pakistan's bilateral exchange rates yields the REER index. Figure 4.4 plots percent changes in REERs for textiles and agriculture as well as for the aggregate country. For added context, the figure also plots these REERs for Cambodia, a country with a similar export profile. Indeed, it was the only one besides Pakistan to appear in both panels of Figure 4.2. The figure ends in 2019 as sector-level price data for 2020 are not yet available.

Owing to the dominance of textiles and agriculture in Pakistan's exports, it is no surprise that its aggregate REER tracks these two closely. However, the two sectors themselves have REERs that are strongly correlated, with both experiencing high appreciation in 2011 and modest depreciation in 2018–2019. This may be concerning since it implies little diversification in Pakistan's export competitiveness. Moreover, the modest depreciations the two sectors registered in 2018–2019 were overshadowed by a much larger depreciation in the aggregate REER, suggesting a boost in overall competitiveness that appears to have been dampened by Pakistan's largest sectors.

Figure 4.4: Change in Real Effective Exchange Rate Index, Pakistan and Cambodia, Selected Sectors, 2010–2019 (%)

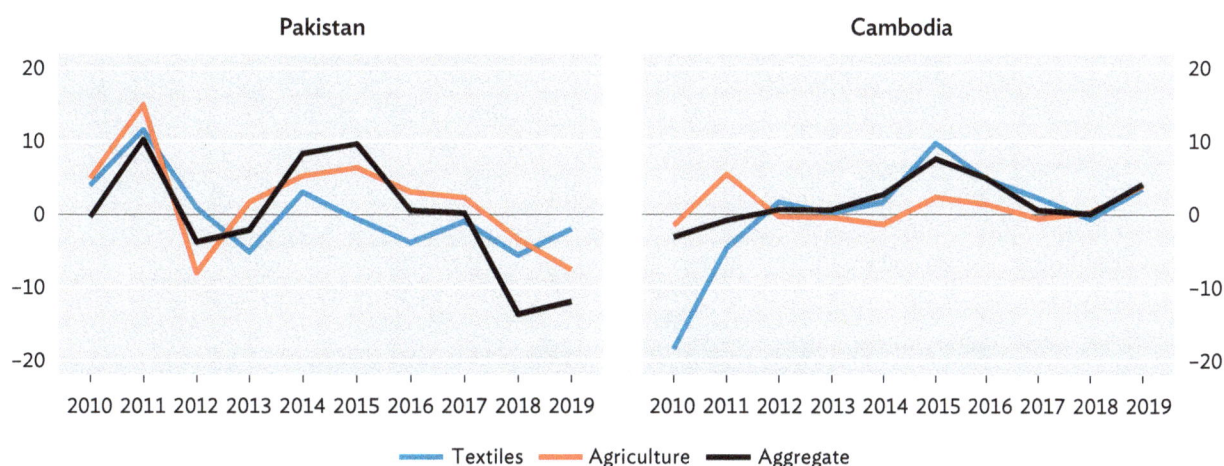

Note: Real effective exchange rate indexes are computed according to Patel, Wang, and Wei (2019).
Sources: Asian Development Bank (ADB). Multiregional Input–Output Database (accessed 1 August 2021); ADB estimates; and S. Patel, Z. Wang, and S. Wei. 2019. Global Value Chains and Effective Exchange Rates at the Country-Sector Level. *Journal of Money, Credit and Banking*. 51 (1). pp. 7–42.

Cambodia's sector-level REERs more tightly track its aggregate REERs, implying that these have an even bigger share in its exports than they do in Pakistan. A key difference between the trends in each country is that Cambodia's have tended to fluctuate less. Notwithstanding a massive depreciation in its textiles REER in 2010, Cambodia's REERs have generally hovered close to zero. This is potentially significant since research suggests that maintaining a stable exchange rate is most conducive to trade (Eichengreen 2008; Rodrik 2008). In the aggregate, the standard deviation in Cambodia's REER change was 3.1 points, while that of Pakistan's was 8.3 points.

To place these numbers into context, Figure 4.5 plots the mean appreciation and standard deviation in aggregate REERs across the 62 countries and economies included in the ADB MRIO database. The period covered is 2010–2019, right after the 2008–2009 global financial crisis and right before the 2020 pandemic, thereby approximating "normal" trading conditions. Stable currencies mean being as close to 0% mean appreciation as possible with low standard deviation, a feat achieved most successfully by Singapore. This stems from having a diverse set of exports and export destinations, which in turn diversifies competitors and minimizes the impact of price changes in each one. On the other end are the commodities-oriented countries of the Russian Federation and Brunei Darussalam, both registering high mean appreciations at high standard deviations. This is no surprise given their heavy reliance on oil exports.

Figure 4.5: Real Effective Exchange Rate Mean and Volatility, 2010–2019 (%)

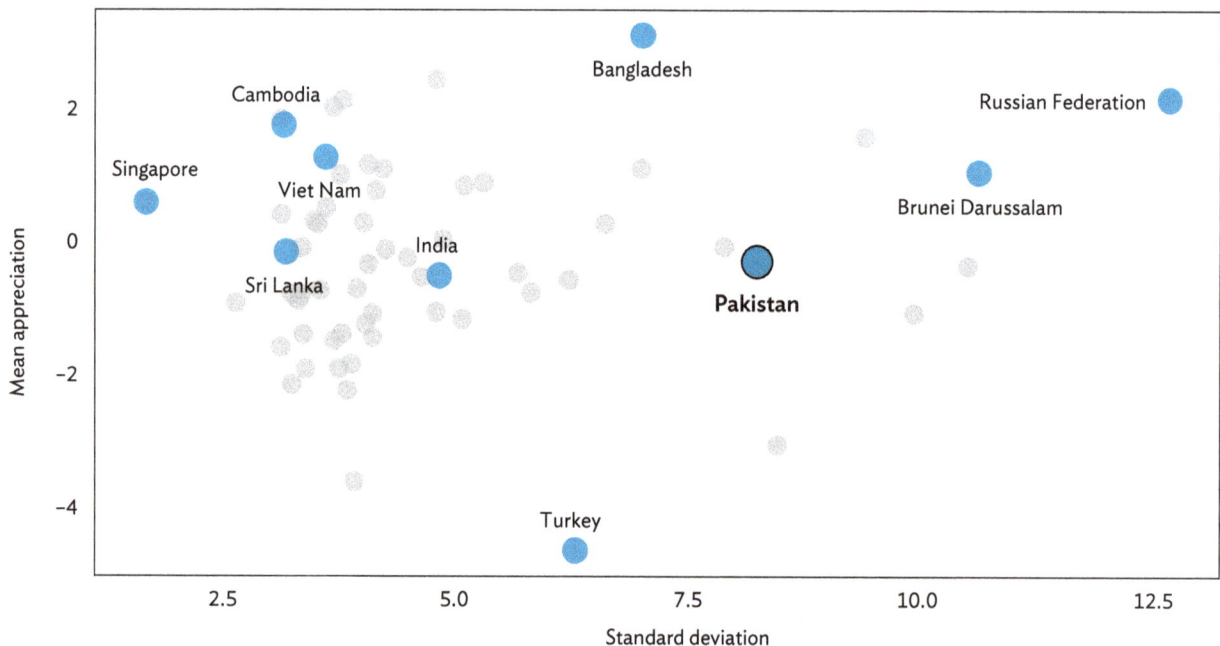

Note: The real effective exchange rate (REER) indexes are computed according to Patel, Wang, and Wei (2019).
Sources: Asian Development Bank (ADB). Multiregional Input–Output Database (accessed 1 August 2021); ADB estimates; and S. Patel, Z. Wang, and S. Wei. 2019. Global Value Chains and Effective Exchange Rates at the Country-Sector Level. *Journal of Money, Credit and Banking.* 51 (1). pp. 7–42.

Among the countries most similar to Pakistan, Cambodia, Viet Nam, and Sri Lanka all have fairly low volatilities, while Bangladesh has high volatility with very high mean appreciation. India is somewhere in the middle. Pakistan itself, though it is close to zero mean appreciation, registered among the highest standard deviations in the entire sample. This makes any effort to expand its external sector more challenging.

To conclude, the RCA index, coupled with GVC production lengths, shows that Pakistan specializes in the downstream segments of textiles and the upstream segments of agriculture. The case for agriculture only emerges when using the value-added version of the RCA, suggesting that exported value added is mostly embodied in exports from other sectors. Pakistan's main competitors in the textiles and agriculture sectors are the domestic producers in its top export destinations, namely the United States, the PRC, and Europe. The value-added-adjusted REER index shows that price competitiveness in these sectors has experienced volatile swings over 2010–2019. Indeed, its aggregate REER is found to have had among the highest volatilities in 62 countries and economies. Given this, greater efforts to maintain a stable and competitive exchange rate must be undertaken.

Chapter 5
SPECIAL TOPICS

This chapter covers some further issues relating to Pakistan's economy and trade, with a focus on global value chains (GVCs). In the first section, its membership in the South Asian Association for Regional Cooperation (SAARC) is analyzed using a regional concentration index and visualized via a skyline chart. The objective is to measure how deep this regional trade agreement is and in what sectors, using both gross and value-added flows.

In the second section, the strength and nature of domestic linkages are explored. These add a layer of complexity in Pakistan's GVC engagement. In the final section, Pakistan's performance during the coronavirus disease (COVID-19) pandemic is investigated. In particular, the question of whether GVCs mitigated or exacerbated the pandemic-induced shock across economies is explored using both a simple correlation and an input–output-based counterfactual exercise.

The South Asian Association for Regional Cooperation

As globalization picked up pace in the 1990s, so did initiatives to deepen and regulate trade on a regional basis. Notwithstanding the success of multilateral initiatives like the creation of the World Trade Organization (WTO) in 1995, negotiating regional trade agreements (RTAs) remained less challenging given the fewer stakeholders involved and the greater immediacy of its benefits (WTO 2011; Limão 2016). During this period, the North American Free Trade Agreement (NAFTA) was formed and the free trade areas of the European Union and the Association of Southeast Asian Nations (ASEAN), among others, were substantially expanded. RTA initiatives continued into and after the 2010s, with the signing of the Comprehensive and Progressive Agreement for Trans-Pacific Partnership and the Regional Comprehensive Economic Partnership.

Pakistan did not sit out this wave of regionalism. Beginning in the 1980s, the countries of South Asia began to abandon the import substitution policies they had followed since independence in favor of trade liberalization, establishing the SAARC in 1985 to promote dialogue. Through the SAARC, the South Asian Preferential Trade Area was established in 1995 and expanded into the South Asian Free Trade Area in 2006 (Baysan, Panagariya, and Pitigala 2006). The SAARC's present members include Afghanistan, Bangladesh, Bhutan, India, Maldives, Nepal, Pakistan, and Sri Lanka. Elsewhere, Pakistan has also been active in the Central Asia Regional Economic Cooperation (CAREC) Program, a partnership founded in 2001 among 11 countries. Its focus has been on regional investments and policy initiatives. Because SAARC is better represented in the ADB MRIO database than CAREC, the succeeding analysis focuses on SAARC.

A common way of measuring the extent of regional trade integration is to take the share of intraregional trade in the region's total trade (exports plus imports). This has been criticized by Frankel (1997), who argues that such a share monotonically increases as the number of members goes up. He proposes normalizing this by the share of the region in world trade, a methodology detailed in Box 7. To illustrate, the intraregional trade share of the 27-member European Union was 52% in 2020, compared with 4.3% for the eight-member SAARC, suggesting the European Union is over 12 times more integrated than the SAARC. However, the European Union takes up 31% of world trade against the SAARC's 2.7%. Thus, the countries of the European Union trade among themselves 1.7 times more than they do with the world, while the SAARC countries trade among themselves 1.6 times more. These two numbers, called regional concentration indexes (RCIs), are now more directly comparable.

Box 7: Calculating the Regional Concentration Index

The regional concentration index (RCI) measures the extent to which a collection of countries (a "region") is trading among themselves relative to the rest of the world. Following Frankel (1997), it is computed as a ratio of two fractions: the share of the region's trade with itself and the share of the region in world trade. Formally, the RCI for region is given by

$$RCI_q = \frac{Exports_{qq} + Imports_{qq}}{Exports_q + Imports_q} \bigg/ \frac{Exports_q + Imports_q}{Exports_{world} + Imports_{world}}$$

Note that $Exports_{qq} = Imports_{qq}$ and $Exports_{world} = Imports_{world}$. That is, the exports of a region to itself is necessarily equal to its imports from itself.

A random collection of countries would have an RCI of close to 1, meaning they trade among each other at about the same rate they trade with the world. If the collection is, for example, geographically close, or share cultural ties, or belong to a deep trade agreement, its RCI would be higher than 1. Conversely, an RCI below 1 means trade within the region is less significant than trade outside it.

Because of international production sharing, the RCI based on gross exports may misstate regional integration in two ways. First, exports may contain value added from outside the region. Second, reexporting by the region's members may result in regional value added actually being absorbed outside the region. To correct for these, an adjusted RCI is also computed that accounts for value added from beginning to end, ensuring that regional flows are truly regional. This is called the end-to-end RCI.

Source: J. A. Frankel. 1997. *Regional Trading Blocs in the World Economic System*. Washington, DC: Peterson Institute for International Economics.

The RCIs for four RTAs are plotted in Figure 5.1. The RCIs on the left panel use gross exports to measure regional integration. These show that among the four, SAARC has tended to have the lowest integration, registering an RCI of 1.6 in 2020. On average, the most integrated region was NAFTA, though in 2019–2020 it was overtaken by a sudden rise in ASEAN integration from 2.0 to 2.5. Finally, the European Union, being the most institutionally mature of the group, exhibited the most stable RCI, hovering between 1.5 and 2.0.

Figure 5.1: Regional Concentration Indexes, Selected Regional Trade Agreements, 2000, 2007–2020

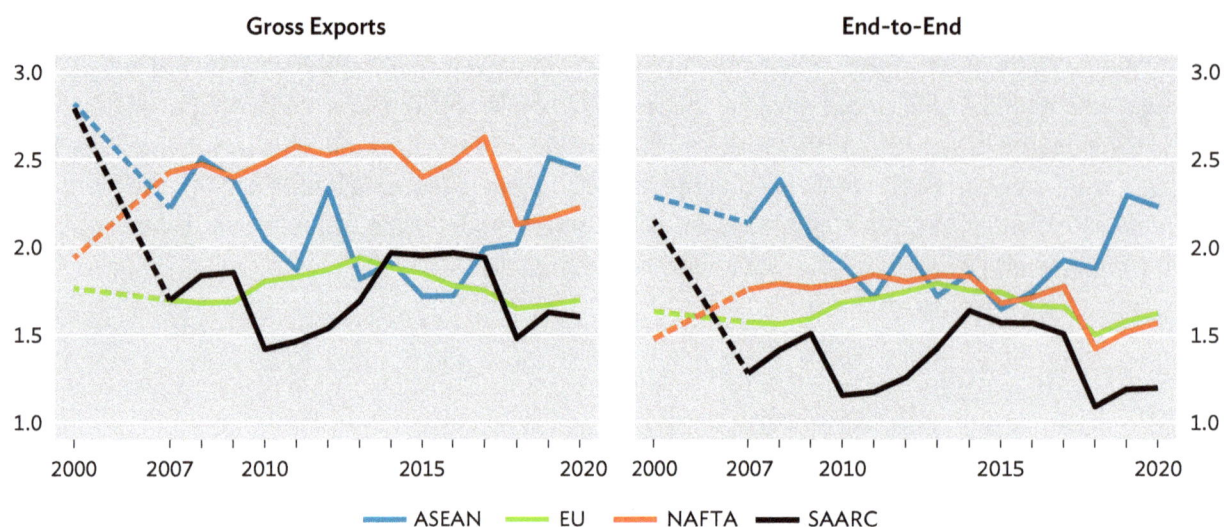

ASEAN = Association of Southeast Asian Nations, EU = European Union, NAFTA = North American Free Trade Agreement, SAARC = South Asian Association for Regional Cooperation.
Notes: Groupings are missing some members if they are not identified in the Asian Development Bank Multiregional Input–Output Database. ASEAN includes Brunei Darussalam, Cambodia, Indonesia, the Lao People's Democratic Republic, Malaysia, the Philippines, Singapore, Thailand, and Viet Nam. EU includes Austria, Belgium, Bulgaria, Croatia, Cyprus, Czech Republic, Denmark, Estonia, Finland, France, Georgia, Germany, Greece, Hungary, Ireland, Italy, Latvia, Lithuania, Luxembourg, the Netherlands, Poland, Portugal, Romania, Slovak Republic, Slovenia, Spain, and Sweden. NAFTA includes Canada, Mexico, and the United States. SAARC includes Bangladesh, Bhutan, Sri Lanka, India, Maldives, Nepal, and Pakistan.
Sources: Asian Development Bank (ADB). Multiregional Input–Output Database (accessed 1 August 2021); and ADB estimates.

As explained in Box 7, using gross exports to calculate the RCI may be misleading due to imported inputs on the one hand and reexporting on the other. In other words, value added from outside the region may be mixed in, a possibility that is all the more relevant in the age of GVCs. Thus, an "end-to-end" RCI that traces value added from creation to final consumption is also presented in Figure 5.1. Perhaps because of South Asia's relatively low GVC participation, the trend of its RCI is almost identical to the gross exports version. SAARC remains the least integrated of the four RTAs. Elsewhere, the high integration of NAFTA disappears, placing it at about the level of the European Union. This suggests that much of what appears to be intra-NAFTA trade actually involves much outside value added.

One interesting observation about SAARC's RCI is that, in either version, it was much higher in 2000 than in the years after its free trade area took effect in 2006. This, however, stems not so much from higher regional integration in the past but rather from a lack of engagement with the rest of the world. Looking at the formula in Box 7, it is clear that the RCI may go up if either the share of intraregional trade goes up (the numerator) or the region's share in world trade goes down (the denominator). Using gross exports, one finds that while intraregional trade in the SAARC remained stable between 2000 and 2007 at 3.2%, its share in world trade went up from 1.2% to 1.9%. Hence the drop in its RCI from 2.8 to 1.7.

Turning to the sector level, regional integration may be visualized with a skyline chart, whose construction is described in Box 8. It represents each sector as a "tower" whose width is its share in the region's output and whose height is its output expressed as a share of the portion induced by domestic demand. A region measuring the output suppressed due to imports is also indicated. The skyline chart's main purpose is to show where the region is self-sufficient in, these being the sectors for which its own internal demand is enough to exhaust its output.

Box 8: Constructing the Skyline Chart

The skyline chart visualizes the industrial structure of an economy and the extent to which it relies on imports (METI, 2011; WTO, 2011b). Each sector is represented by a "tower," as in the figure. The width of the tower measures the share of that sector in the economy's output. The height of the tower measures output induced by demand for that sector, computed using data from an input–output table. Output induced by domestic demand is normalized at 100%, with anything above it corresponding to output induced by export demand. Part of the tower is shaded red to indicate the reduction in output induced by imports, which, being negative, starts from the top of the tower and extends downward.

If the blue region of the tower is above the 100% line, then the sector it represents is said to be self-sufficient. That is, its own output is enough to satisfy its induced domestic demand. If it is below the 100% line, however, then domestic output is insufficient and the economy has had to import the shortfall in supply. The actual height of the blue region is called the sector's self-sufficiency ratio.

In this chapter, the skyline chart is constructed at the regional level. Thus, the underlying input–output table is aggregated at the regional level. This means that imports and exports now refer to flows going in and out of the region, while flows between economies within the region are treated as "domestic" flows. Self-sufficiency then refers to the ability of the region to supply its induced demand without having to import from outside the region.

A Tower in a Skyline Chart

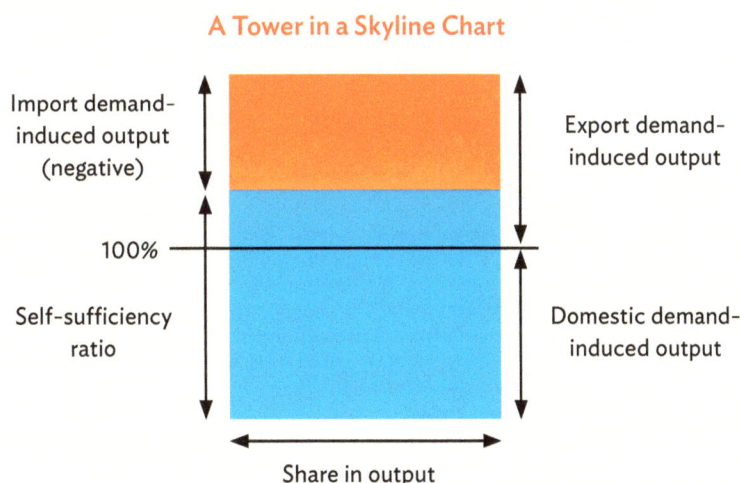

Import demand-induced output (negative)

Export demand-induced output

100%

Self-sufficiency ratio

Domestic demand-induced output

Share in output

Source: Authors' drawing based on World Trade Organization (2011b).

Sources:
Government of Japan, Ministry of Economy, Trade and Industry (METI). 2011. *White Paper on International Economy and Trade*. Supplementary Notes.
World Trade Organization (WTO). 2011a. *World Trade Report 2011—The WTO and Preferential Trade Agreements: From Co-Existence to Coherence*. Geneva.
WTO. 2011b. *Trade Patterns and Global Value Chains in East Asia: From Trade in Goods to Trade in Tasks*. Geneva.

The skyline chart for SAARC using 2020 data is presented in Figure 5.2. The economic structure of its members is evident in the large shares attributable to agriculture, for which the region is just about self-sufficient in. Its most export-oriented sector is unsurprisingly textiles, for which output is 1.5 times the amount the region demands. Another major sector is "other business activities", though this is likely driven solely by India, whose business process outsourcing sector is a global powerhouse.

Figure 5.2: Skyline Chart for the South Asian Association for Regional Cooperation Countries, 2020

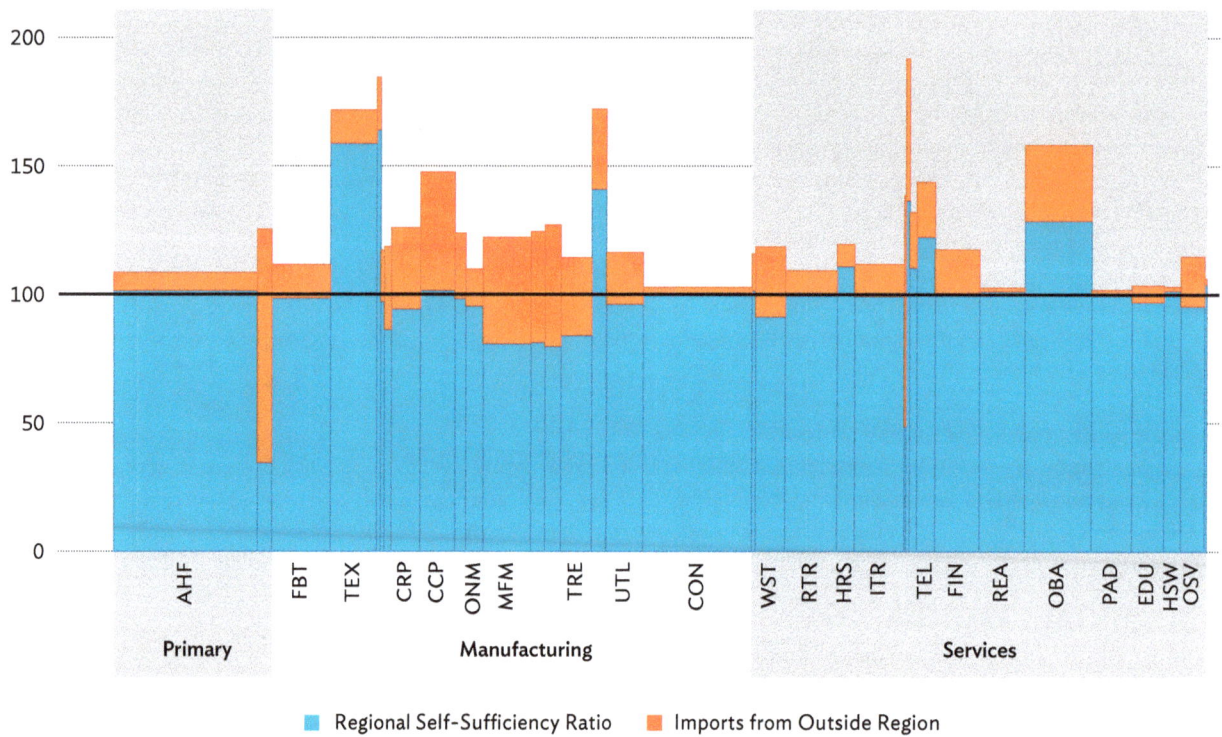

Legend: ■ Regional Self-Sufficiency Ratio   ■ Imports from Outside Region

AHF = agriculture, hunting, forestry, and fishing; CCP = chemicals and chemical products; CON = construction; CRP = coke, refined petroleum, and nuclear fuel; EDU = education; EOE = electrical and optical equipment; FBT = food, beverages, and tobacco; FIN = financial intermediation; HRS = hotels and restaurants; HSW = health and social work; ITR = inland transport; MCH = machinery, not elsewhere classified; MFM = basic metals and fabricated metal; OBA = renting of machinery and equipment and other business activities; ONM = other nonmetallic mineral; OSV = other community, social, and personal services; PAD = public administration and defense; compulsory social security; REA = real estate activities; RTR = retail trade and repair, except of motor vehicles and motorcycles; TEL = post and telecommunications; TEX = textiles and textile products; TRE = transport equipment; UTL = electricity, gas, and water supply; WST = wholesale trade, except of motor vehicles and motorcycles.
Notes: The South Asian Association for Regional Cooperation includes Afghanistan, Bangladesh, Bhutan, Sri Lanka, India, the Maldives, Nepal, and Pakistan. However, Afghanistan is excluded from the chart due to missing data.
Sources: Asian Development Bank (ADB). Multiregional Input–Output Database (accessed 1 August 2021); and ADB estimates.

Apart from textiles, construction, and some other relatively small sectors, SAARC's manufacturing demand is dependent on imports. Its output in metals, electricals, transport equipment, and other machinery meet just 80% of its own demand, a far cry from the surpluses generated in other regions like ASEAN who use these exports to fuel growth. While textiles have come to serve this function for the SAARC countries, their role in this sector has remained in the relatively low-value-adding segments (see Chapter 3). Figure 5.2, then, provides a clear picture of the challenges facing SAARC should it strive for a larger export sector.

Agglomeration

Domestic linkages add a layer of complexity in a country's role in GVCs. In a highly integrated global economy, domestic sectors contribute either through intermediate inputs later consumed by other sectors or through a domestic sector's demand for inputs from other sectors. However, indicators of GVCs do not typically capture the indirect contribution of domestic sectors (Mercer-Blackman et al. 2017; Bernard et al. 2007).

In Pakistan, domestic linkages play a significant role. As shown in Chapter 2, the country is less integrated in global production networks relative to its regional neighbors (see also State Bank of Pakistan 2020). Most production activities remain concentrated in the domestic market, a result of policies that seek to increase domestic value added (DVA) in the economy (Dollar et al. 2020). For example, Pakistan's tariff structure is designed to promote exports in key sectors while protecting local industries, incentivizing manufacturers to source their inputs locally (Nasir 2020).

Pakistan's textile industry illustrates the concentration of activities in the domestic economy. Like Bangladesh, textiles are the largest exporting sector in Pakistan. Despite this, the performance of the sector differs between the two countries. The DVA for the textiles sector in Pakistan was at 80% in 2016, in contrast to 64.5% of Bangladesh. However, exports of textiles in Bangladesh exhibit a higher growth rate compared to Pakistan (Dollar et al. 2020).

The dominance of DVA for Pakistan's textiles sector arises from barriers to trade. Tariffs on intermediates are at 8%, four times higher than that of East Asia's average. High tariffs discourage the imports of intermediate inputs. While there are existing tax concessions for selected sectors in imported inputs, availing these concessions remain difficult in practice (Nasir 2020; World Bank 2020). It is not surprising, therefore, to find that textiles exporters in Pakistan continue to rely on domestic sources for their inputs (World Bank 2020).

The economic implications of domestic linkages are not straightforward. On the one hand, strong domestic linkages imply spillovers from sectors interlinked with the rest of the world to sectors whose activities are mostly concentrated in the home country. Thus, strong domestic linkages are associated with gains from participating in GVCs (Banga 2014). On the other hand, strong domestic linkages may result from policies that encourage sectors to source inputs from the domestic economy. This, in turn, implies less reliance in international trade, resulting in a "reshoring" of activities back to the domestic economy.

Developing a measure of domestic linkages becomes critical in examining how concentration of economic activities in the domestic economy evolves, on the aggregate and at a sector level. Earlier measures use output multipliers to measure the strength of domestic linkages (Jones 2011; Bartelme and Gorodnichenko 2015). More recent measures use either the imported inputs ratio in the manufacturing sector or the indirect value added in exports (Kearney 2021; Tang, Wei, and Wang 2020). However, these are either limited to specific sectors or challenging to implement.

This section adapts the concept of agglomeration for GVCs by measuring domestic linkages as the tendency of economic activities to "locate" domestically. Specifically, the proposed agglomeration index measures how much value added is sourced from and/or absorbed by domestic sectors relative to the rest of the world. A discussion on how the index is constructed is provided in Box 9.

Box 9: Constructing the Agglomeration Index

Assume that $\mathbf{v}$ is the vector of value-added coefficients and $\mathbf{y}^d$ the vector of domestic final good sales. Denote $\mathbf{A}^d$ as the matrix of domestic technical coefficients and $\mathbf{B}^d = (\mathbf{I} - \mathbf{A}^d)^{-1}$. Then

$$V^D = \hat{\mathbf{v}}\mathbf{B}^d\,\mathbf{y}^d$$

is the vector of value-added generated in each country-sector that ends up as final goods absorbed domestically, while

$$Y^D = \mathbf{v}\mathbf{B}^d\,\hat{\mathbf{y}}^d$$

is the vector of each country-sector's final goods absorbed domestically whose value added also originated domestically. A hat on top of a vector, as in $\hat{\mathbf{x}}$, denotes its diagonalized version.

Let $\mathbf{va}$ be the vector of value added generated by each country-sector. The forward agglomeration index for country-sector (s,i) is given by

$$AGG^B_{s,i} = \frac{Y^D_{(s,i)}/y_{(s,i)}}{\sum^t_{\tau=t-1}\sum_r \gamma_{(r,i,\tau)} Y^D_{(r,i,\tau)}/2y_{(r,i,\tau)}}.$$

The numerator is the share of value added generated in (s,i) that ends up as final goods absorbed domestically in total value added generated in (s,i). The denominator is the 2-year moving average of the same share for sector i for all countries, using sector share ($\gamma_{(r,i,\tau)}$) as weights. Thus, the forward agglomeration index is the ratio of (s,i)'s V^D share against the world average for that sector.

Likewise, let $\mathbf{y}$ be the vector of final good sales by each country-sector. The backward agglomeration index for country-sector (s,i) is given by

$$AGG^B_{s,i} = \frac{Y^D_{(s,i)}/y_{(s,i)}}{\sum^t_{\tau=t-1}\sum_r \gamma_{(r,i,\tau)} Y^D_{(r,i,\tau)}/2y_{(r,i,\tau)}}.$$

This is the ratio of (s,i)'s Y^D share in final goods sales against the world average for that sector.

continued on next page.

Box 9 *continued.*

Being ratios, agglomeration in either perspective is said to be high if the index is greater than 1; conversely, if it were less than 1. A country-sector may be profiled by whether it has high or low forward and backward agglomeration. The four possible types are presented in the agglomeration map below.

The Agglomeration Map

Reshoring economies $AGG^F < 1, AGG^B > 1$	High agglomeration $AGG^F > 1, AGG^B > 1$
Low agglomeration $AGG^F < 1, AGG^B < 1$	DVA generating economies $AGG^F > 1, AGG^B < 1$

Source: Authors' drawing.

A high backward agglomeration signals that domestic value added embodied in final goods and services consumed domestically is high. Intuitively, this imply that domestic production for domestic consumption is higher than the world average. Meanwhile, a high forward agglomeration indicates that domestic sectors absorb a significant portion of value added generated by a country-sector. This means that value added that goes to domestic production is higher than world average. The classification presented in the agglomeration map combine these two effects to determine the form of domestic linkages taking place in a country-sector.

Source: V. Mercer-Blackman, A. Foronda, and M. J. Mariasingham. 2017. Using Input–Output Analysis Framework to Explain Economic Diversification and Structural Transformation in Bangladesh. *ADB Economics Working Paper Series*. No. 513. Manila: Asian Development Bank.

The agglomeration indexes allow for an analysis of how concentrated economic activities are in Pakistan relative to other countries. Focus is given to neighboring ADB MRIO countries, namely Bangladesh, India, the PRC, and Sri Lanka. Both the backward and forward agglomeration indexes have been higher in Pakistan across the years (Figure 5.3). High backward agglomeration implies that domestic production for domestic consumption is high, which may be attributed to barriers to trade. For example, tariff rates in Pakistan and Bangladesh are highest in the region from 2007 to 2017.[4] This, in turn, incentivizes reliance on the domestic sector for sourcing inputs, resulting in high backward agglomeration. It must be noted, however, that Pakistan's backward agglomeration has declined over time in contrast to the rest of the region.

Meanwhile, a high forward agglomeration signals that value added absorbed domestically as final goods and services in Pakistan is higher compared to other countries. Thus, on average, sectors in Pakistan generate more value added to domestic sectors compared to the rest of the region.

The agglomeration indexes allow for a deeper analysis of domestic concentration at a sector level. Using the ADB MRIO sector classification, Figure 5.4 plots the agglomeration indexes for the textiles sector in 2010 and 2019. Pakistan is compared to Bangladesh, Cambodia, India, and Sri Lanka, who contribute significantly to textiles exports in the world. The indexes are plotted in the agglomeration map, which examines (i) the level of agglomeration in the textile sector of different countries, and (ii) the movement of the textile sector across different agglomeration classes over time.

---

4   World Bank. Tcdata360 (accessed 29 September 2021).

Figure 5.3: Backward and Forward Agglomeration Indexes, 2007, 2010, and 2019

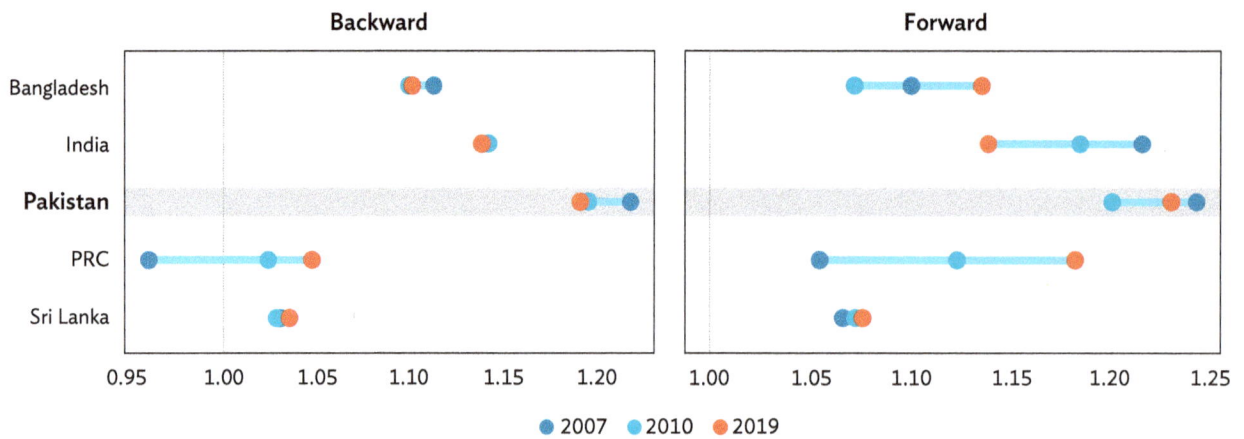

Backward

Forward

● 2007 ● 2010 ● 2019

PRC = People's Republic of China.
Source: Asian Development Bank. Multiregional Input–Output Database (accessed 1 August 2021)

Figure 5.4: Agglomeration Map, Textiles, 2010 and 2019

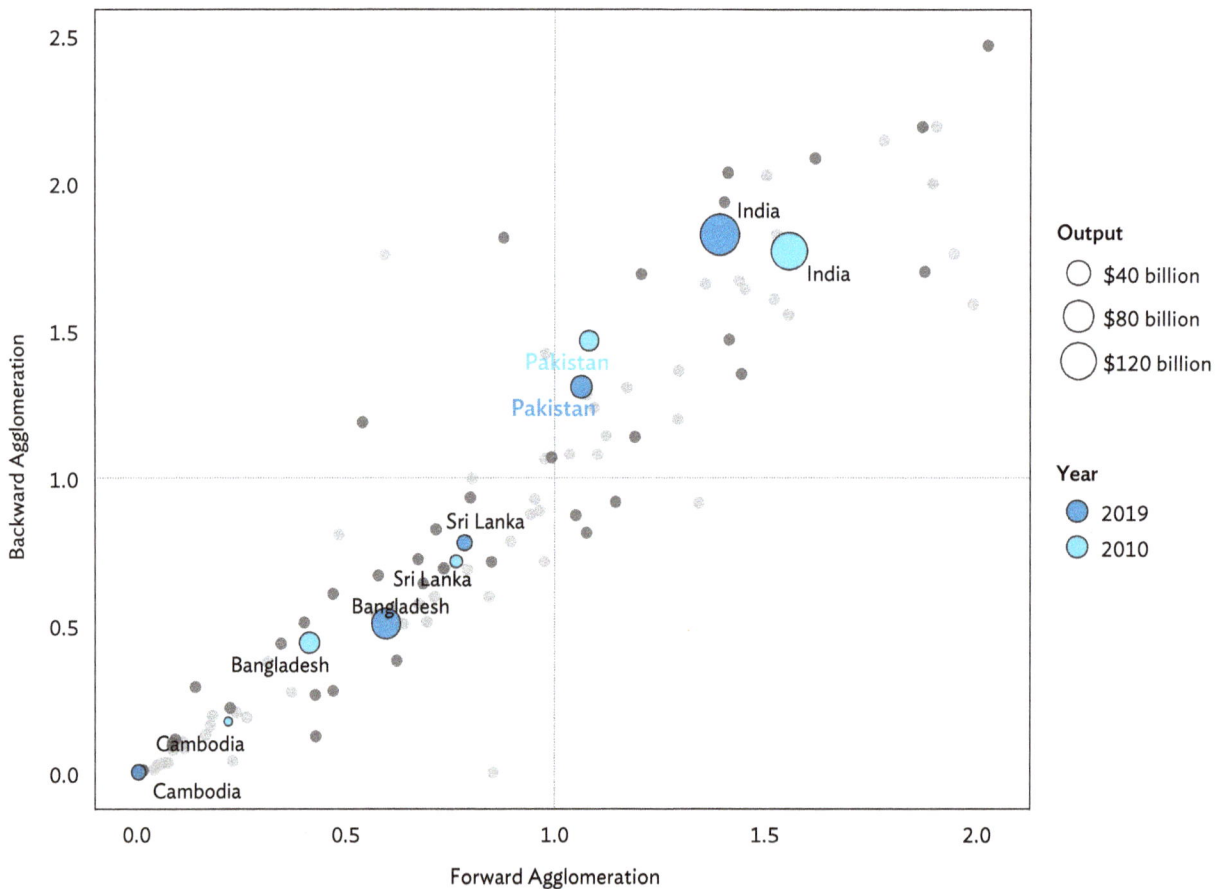

Source: Asian Development Bank. Multiregional Input–Output Database (accessed 1 August 2021).

Among the sample of selected countries, Pakistan and India belong to the high agglomeration class in the last decade. This implies high backward and forward agglomeration in the textiles sector of both countries. Other countries, such as Bangladesh, Cambodia, and Sri Lanka, are consistently in the low agglomeration class—i.e., for these countries, the value added that textiles sector sources from and/or forwards to domestic sectors are lower than the world average.

A decline in backward agglomeration is observed for Pakistan between 2010 and 2019. Hence, the textiles sector is starting to rely less on domestic sectors as a source of inputs. Meanwhile, forward agglomeration exhibits very little change for Pakistan's textiles sector and remains to be high (AGG^F >1). Thus, the value added generated by Pakistan's textiles sector that is absorbed domestically as final goods is higher compared to the rest of the world.

Overall, this illustrates that Pakistan's textiles sector exhibits strong domestic linkages, which are evolving overtime. The decline in backward agglomeration for Pakistan's textiles sector may signal that Pakistan is starting to rely less on domestic sectors as sources of intermediates. Strong forward agglomeration, on the other hand, depicts ability of domestic sectors to absorb value added from GVCs, increasing incentives to participate. Whether this marks the start of a period of increased integration to GVCs for Pakistan remains to be seen.

The COVID-19 Shock

The COVID-19 pandemic that began in 2020 set off unprecedented disruptions to economic activity and trade. While the full extent of its consequences will take years to unfold, preliminary data in the ADB MRIO dataset provide a glimpse into one facet of the crisis: the role of GVCs. By connecting countries to other markets in complex ways, GVCs have the power to both mitigate shocks (through diversification) and amplify shocks (though contagion effects). Which effect dominates will depend on the circumstances prevailing in a given country (ADB 2021).

As a first approximation of the impact of GVCs on COVID-19 outcomes, this section correlates each country's GVC participation in 2019 with the shock to GDP it experienced in 2020. The GVC participation is measured by the share of indirect trade in exports (see Box 3), lagged by 1 year to remove potential distortions that occurred during the pandemic. The measure for the COVID-19 shock to GDP uses the difference in forecasted and actual growth rates for 2020, the reasoning being that this reflects the unexpected disruptions of the pandemic. Box 10 provides more details.

Box 10: Estimating the COVID-19 Shock

The coronavirus disease (COVID-19) shock is defined as the percentage-point deviation in the growth of a macroeconomic variable attributable to the unexpected disruptions caused by the pandemic. That is, if GDP growth contracted by 5% in 2020 where it would have grown by 5% had there been no pandemic, then the COVID-19 shock was negative 10 percentage points.

Of course, counterfactual growth rates are impossible to know for certain, but a reasonable approximation, used in research like Giglioli et al. (2021), are pre-2020 forecasts. Growth forecasts for a country reflect all available information at the moment they are made, so any deviation from them would be shocks in the truest sense—that is, random fluctuations with an expected value of zero. By comparing forecasts made just before the onset of the pandemic with actual growth rates in 2020, an estimate of the COVID-19 shock is obtained.

In this section, forecasts for gross domestic product growth are taken from the October 2019 edition of the International Monetary Fund's *World Economic Outlook* (IMF 2019).

Sources:
S. Giglioli, G. Giovannetti, E. Marvasi, and A. Vivoli. 2021. The Resilience of Global Value Chains During the Covid-19 Pandemic: The Case of Italy. *UniFI DISEI Working Papers – Economics*. No. 07/2021. Florence, Italy: Università degli Studi Firenze Dipartimento di Scienze per L'Economia e L'Impresa.
International Monetary Fund. 2019. *World Economic Outlook, October 2019: Global Manufacturing Downturn, Rising Trade Barriers*. Washington, DC.

Figure 5.5 plots these two variables for the 62 countries covered in the ADB MRIO database. A quadratic line is fitted through them along with its 95% confidence interval. What emerges is an inverted-U relationship, where the size of the COVID-19 shock increases (i.e., becomes more negative) the higher the GVC participation rate up to a rate of about 45%, after which the shock decreases the higher the participation rate.

Pakistan had the lowest GVC participation rate in the dataset at 25.4%. Tellingly, its COVID-19 shock was a relatively mild at –2.8 points, meaning growth in 2020 was 2.8 percentage points lower than what it would have been without the pandemic. This compares favorably with a country like the Philippines, whose GVC participation was much higher at 47.1% and whose shock was also much higher at –15.7 points.

On the flip side, those economies with the highest rates of GVC participation appeared to have done relatively well. The most dramatic case is Taipei,China, whose participation rate was 57.5% and whose shock was actually positive at 1.2 points, meaning the pandemic's disruptions seemed to have made it grow faster. Elsewhere, Viet Nam, with a participation rate of 58.8%, experienced a shock of –3.6 points.

As the figure shows, there is much variation around the average relationship. Indeed, both the Philippines and Taipei,China are far away from the fitted curve, suggesting that a host of other factors contributed to influencing the size of the shock. Nevertheless, the U-shaped relationship is distinct. One explanation may be found in a similar study by Giglioni et al. (2021), who divide 2020 into a "first wave" (October 2019 to April 2020) and a "second wave" (April to October 2020). They find that while GVC participation exacerbated the shock in the first wave, its impact was positive-to-neutral in the second wave. By taking 2020 as a whole, Figure 5.5 may be collating these two trends.

Figure 5.5: The COVID-19 Shock to Growth under Varying Rates of Global Value Chain Participation

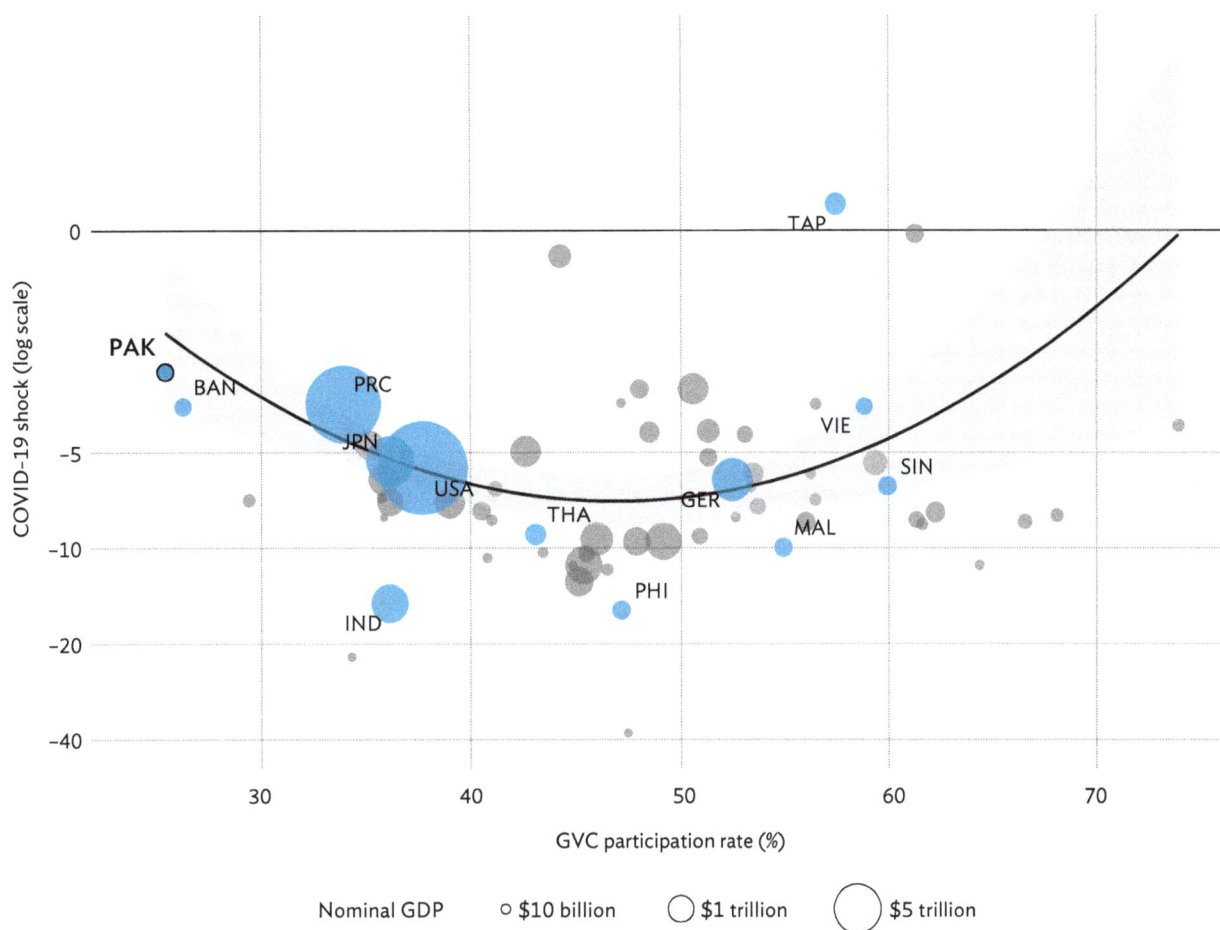

BAN = Bangladesh, COVID-19 = coronavirus disease 2019, IND = India, GDP = gross domestic product, GER = Germany, GVC = global value chain, JPN = Japan, MAL = Malaysia, PAK = Pakistan, PHI = Philippines, PRC = People's Republic of China, TAP = Taipei,China, THA = Thailand, SIN = Singapore, USA = United States, VIE = Viet Nam.

Notes:
1. Participation rates are trade-based rates computed using the methodology in Asian Development Bank (2021). The COVID-19 shock is the percentage-point difference between forecasted gross domestic product growth for 2020 and actual growth in 2020. Participation rates and nominal GDP are as of 2019.
2. Forecasted growth rates from the International Monetary Fund's World Economic Outlook (October 2019) and actual growth rates from the International Monetary Fund's World Economic Outlook (April 2021).

Sources: Asian Development Bank (ADB). 2021. *Key Indicators for Asia and the Pacific 2021*. Manila; ADB. Multiregional Input–Output Database (accessed 1 August 2021); International Monetary Fund (IMF). 2019. *World Economic Outlook, October 2019: Global Manufacturing Downturn, Rising Trade Barriers*. Washington, DC; and IMF. World Economic Outlook Database: April 2021 edition (accessed 1 August 2021).

As for whether the U-shaped pattern points to some "optimal" level of GVC participation, the given results are unable to give a definitive answer. Even if better data in the coming years would prove that the relationship is robust, there is no guarantee that the unique circumstances of the COVID-19 pandemic generalize to other types of shocks. A better prescription to keep in mind is that trade, in general, must be accompanied by a sound institutional framework that maximizes its benefits while minimizing its costs.

Rather than correlating the output shock with GVC participation, another way to investigate the role of GVCs during the pandemic is to start from the demand shock and use this to estimate the output shock under different degrees of openness. Box 11 outlines how the information in an intercountry input–output table can be used to control the channels by which demand shocks propagate through the world economy.

Box 11: The COVID-19 Shock under Different Trading Scenarios

Input–output analysis allows one to distinguish the channels by which demand shocks impact gross domestic product (GDP). Different scenarios are identified by turning certain channels on and off. The present analysis identifies three:

(i) **Baseline scenario.** This corresponds to real-world conditions, where imported inputs and reexporting within global value chains have connected countries in indirect ways.

(ii) **Classical trading scenario.** Trading occurs, but only directly, i.e., there is no usage of imported inputs and no reexporting. This corresponds to the classical idea of trade commonly assumed in economics textbooks.

(iii) **Autarkic scenario.** No trading occurs.

The coronavirus disease (COVID-19) shock is estimated by the difference in reported final demand for 2020 and forecasts for 2020 made by the World Bank at the start of the year (World Bank 2020). The World Bank has the widest set of final demand forecasts, so its dataset is used here. All other data are derived from the Asian Development Bank multiregional input–output database. Values are in current prices.

Under scenario R, the impact of the COVID-19 shock to the GDP of country s is given by

$$\text{Shock}_s^R = \frac{\text{GDP}_s^R\left(\mathbf{Y}^{\text{actual}}\right) - \text{GDP}_s^R\left(\mathbf{Y}^{\text{forecast}}\right)}{\text{GDP}_s^R\left(\mathbf{Y}^{\text{forecast}}\right)}$$

A comparison of $\text{Shock}_s^{\text{Autarky}}$, $\text{Shock}_s^{\text{Classical}}$, and $\text{Shock}_s^{\text{GVC}}$ provides a heuristic explanation of how the presence of global value chains dampens or intensifies global demand shocks.

Sources:
Asian Development Bank. Multiregional Input–Output Database (accessed 1 August 2021).
World Bank. 2020. *Global Economic Prospects, January 2020: Slow Growth, Policy Challenges*. Washington, DC.

The intuition behind this counterfactual exercise is as follows. Lockdown measures during the pandemic resulted in demand shocks around the world. Each country was exposed to these shocks via three channels: through its own domestic economy, through its direct trading partners, and through its indirect trading partners. Several outcomes are possible. If the shock a country faced from domestic sources was large (severe lockdowns, extreme falls in disposable income) while the shocks it faced from its trading partners were milder (shorter lockdowns, generous government assistance), then open trading channels allow the overall shock to its GDP to be mitigated. On the other hand, if its domestic shock was mild while its trading partners' shocks were severe, then open trading channels worsens the overall shock to its GDP.

Three trading scenarios are considered: baseline, classical trading, and autarky. The baseline scenario corresponds to real-world conditions, where the presence of GVCs means countries may be affected even by demand shocks from sources with whom they have no direct trade with. Classical trading allows only direct trading. That is, there is no usage of imported inputs and no reexporting.[5] Finally, autarky turns off all trading channels.

The top panel of Figure 5.6 plots the percent-changes in nominal GDP following the pandemic-induced demand shock under the three trading scenarios. In Pakistan's case, its GDP falls by 12.4% under the baseline scenario. Turning off indirect trade channels worsens this slightly to −12.5%, while turning off all trade channels brings this to −12.9%. These estimates are not far from each other, likely because Pakistan's exposure to trade, in general, and GVCs, in particular, is not very high to begin with. Nevertheless, looking at the bottom panel, these suggest that without any trade, Pakistan's contraction would have been 0.5 percentage points larger. GVCs were thus able to mitigate some of the effects of the pandemic.

The opposite is the case for other countries. Sri Lanka, for example, is estimated to contract by 10.0% under both the baseline and classical trading scenarios, but only by 8.2% under autarky. An interesting case is Maldives. Under the baseline scenario, its GDP contracts by 27.4%, while under classical trading, this worsens by almost 1 percentage-point to 28.4%. However, under autarky, this shrinks to 26.6%. Thus, moving from a state of autarky to classical trading worsens outcomes severely for the Maldives, but opening its trade further to allow GVCs mitigates these outcomes somewhat.

Figure 5.5 and Figure 5.6 demonstrate what ADB (2021) calls the two faces of GVCs. That is, as far as the available data suggests, exposure to GVCs had both benefits and costs during the COVID-19 pandemic. As countries take advantage of the opportunities GVCs bring, they must also ensure that the accompanying risks are properly accounted for.

---

[5]   Chapter 3 discusses the difference between direct and indirect trading in greater detail.

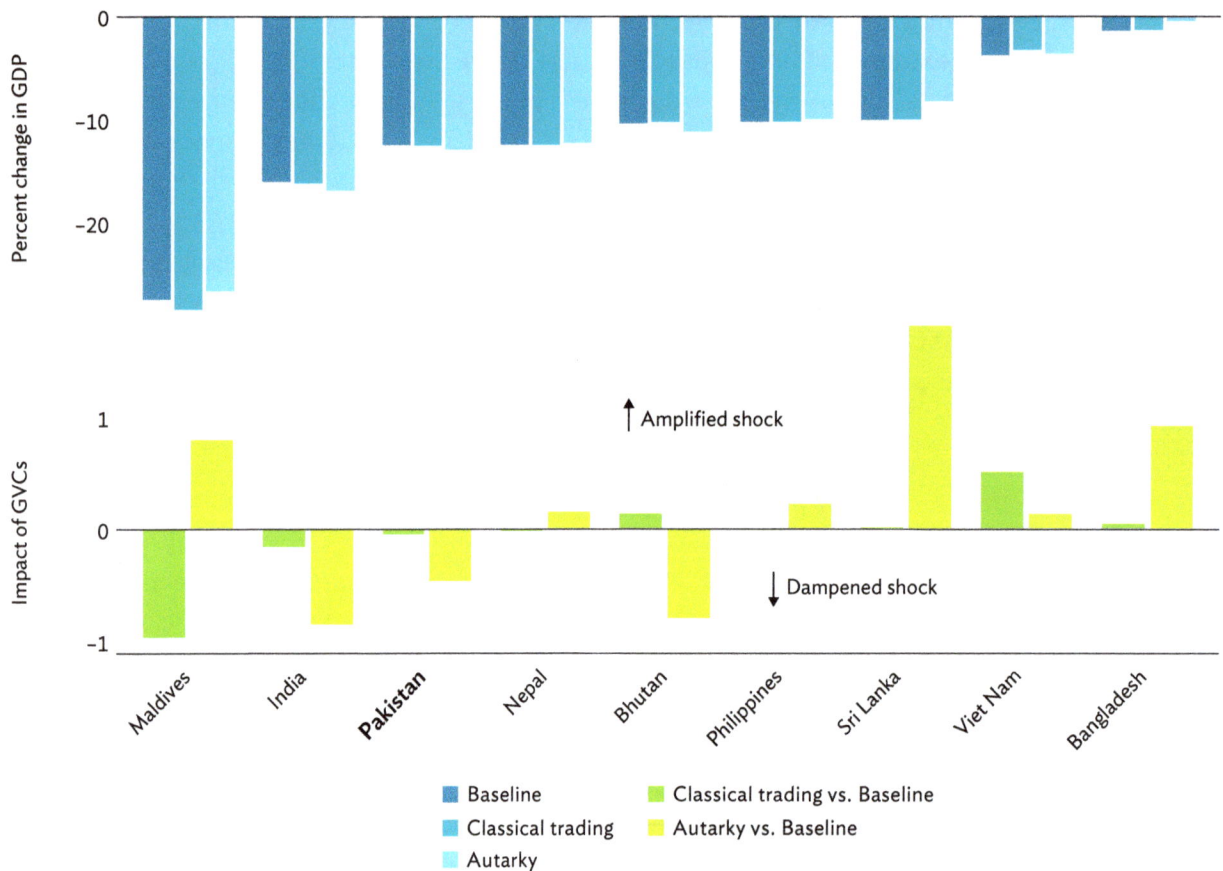

Figure 5.6: The COVID-19 Shock under Different Trade Scenarios, Selected Economies

GDP = gross domestic product, GVC = global value chain.
Notes: The top panel gives the percent change in GDP given the pandemic-induced demand shock under different trade scenarios. "Baseline" assumes all forms of trade and corresponds to the real world. "Classical trading" assumes only direct trade. "Autarky" assumes no trade. The bottom panel is the percentage-point differences of the numbers in the top panel.
Sources: Asian Development Bank (ADB). Multiregional Input–Output Database (accessed 1 August 2021); and ADB estimates.

Chapter 6
CONCLUSION

In its country partnership strategy for Pakistan, ADB (2020a) outlines three strategic pillars its assistance will prioritize over the period 2021–2025:

(i)   improving economic management to restore stability and growth,

(ii)   building resilience through human capital development and social protection to enhance productivity and people's well-being, and

(iii)   boosting competitiveness and private sector development to create jobs and expand economic opportunities.

This report is a knowledge product that complements ADB's country partnership strategy by describing the state of Pakistan economy and its engagement with global value chains (GVCs). It builds its analysis from a combination of up-to-date datasets and the best available analytical tools. By efficiently connecting suppliers to consumers and lowering barriers to entry into high-value industries, GVCs have proven to be a potent stimulus to growth, human capital development, and competitiveness. This report, however, also highlights the risks of GVCs (Figure 5.5 and Figure 5.6). In a more interconnected world, shocks in one place ripple through the system to affect seemingly distant economies. GVC participation, therefore, must be done the right way.

Having among the lowest GVC participation rates in the world (Figure 3.4), the Pakistan economy is primed to benefit enormously from adopting a more outward-oriented development strategy. Provided that it does so in a careful and deliberate manner, Pakistan's already impressive achievements in poverty reduction can be pushed further and its boom-and-bust growth pattern can be put on a more stable trend.

To maximize the benefits and minimize the costs of GVCs, this report recommends the following principles:

Diversification. The key to managing many types of risk is diversification. In the case of GVCs, Pakistan would do well to diversify not just its export basket but also the markets it sells to. In Chapter 2, it was shown that while Pakistan's merchandise exports were generally more diversified than those of Bangladesh and Cambodia, they were still less diverse than India's (Figure 2.5). Moreover, Figure 2.4 pointed to the dominance of textile products. Specialization in this sector is not necessarily an unsound strategy, as demonstrated by the solid growth record of other textiles-heavy exporters like Bangladesh and Cambodia. However, Pakistan must ensure that, within this sector, firms are able to participate all along the productivity spectrum and are not stuck in low-value-added segments (as illustrated in the decomposition of GVC production lengths in Figure 3.7, which indicates that textiles exports rely heavily on processing abroad).

It was also shown in Chapter 2 that Pakistan maintains a fairly diverse set of trading partners, which includes the United States, Europe, and the PRC for its textiles and the Middle East for its rice. Figure 3.2 also showed that export destinations and foreign value-added sources were spread out across many countries when looked at by value-added category. Nevertheless, with a trade-to-GDP ratio of 30%, Pakistan's producers are in effect highly concentrated in a single market: its own. Greater trade participation will in itself diversify the country's sources of demand and is a strategy worth exploring from a risk management perspective.

Investing in people. Using government census data for 2017, World Bank (2020a) paints a concerning picture of the state of human capital in Pakistan. Almost 60% of the labor force are either uneducated or completed only primary education, with the out-of-school population numbering some 20 million–25 million. Of 1,000 live births, about 75 children die before the age of 5, the highest rate in South Asia. Among those who live, over one-third are stunted. Access to education and health services is vastly unequal. Moreover, all these conditions have been made more challenging by the COVID-19 pandemic.

Apart from its worthy contribution to welfare, investing in human capital yields significant economic returns when paired with the opportunities provided by GVCs. The services sector is already a proven driver of poverty reduction in Pakistan, albeit largely through the informal economy. Such talent can be turned to more productive employment in the global business process outsourcing industry. Indeed, the experiences of India and the Philippines have shown that manufacturing need no longer be synonymous with an export-led development strategy. Services, too, can fill this function, with the bonus of generally having lower fixed capital requirements. This can serve to complement Pakistan's textiles sector.

Institutional support. The set of institutional frameworks prevailing in a country greatly influences its economy. These may be divided into those that deal with enlarging the economic pie and those that deal with how that pie is shared. To enlarge the pie, the government can focus on the collection of general growth-promoting policies discussed in the last principle below. Redistributing the pie, however, will involve more country-specific concerns. Opening up to GVCs tends to cause temporary disruptions as the existing stock of skills adjusts to the actual skills demanded by the world economy. There will be winners and losers, at least in the short term. Policies must be designed to ensure that no group suffers too great a drop in welfare and that all have a path to participating gainfully in the external sector. Moreover, since good policy design requires plenty of timely information, institutional support must also be given to data-collecting agencies. Indeed, such support was needed to construct the input–output tables that much of this report was based on.

Multilateral engagement. Trade can only thrive in a stable, rules-based global environment where competition is as free and as fair as possible. As such, it is in Pakistan's interest to strengthen multilateral bodies like the WTO and the SAARC. It must actively participate not only in crafting their rules but also in enforcing them. Moreover, Pakistan must continue to pursue new trade agreements through which it can lower barriers to trade, exchange information, and establish mutual trust. International cooperation can also help Pakistan address trade-adjacent issues that require collective action such as climate change, migration, and conflict. Such initiatives will also aid in the principles of diversification and institutional support described above.

Remembering the basics. Beyond GVCs, the usual set of principles that promote a robust and dynamic economy must not be neglected. The population must be healthy and educated, as already mentioned above. To efficiently move people and goods around the country, sustained investments in physical infrastructure and information and communications technologies are necessary. Financial markets must be inclusive and well-developed, with mechanisms to deal with defaults that do not unduly punish risk-taking. Property rights must be secure. Workers, entrepreneurs, and investors alike must have faith in an impartial court system dedicated to the rule of law. Labor and redistribution policies must be studied thoroughly to ensure that they achieve what they are meant to achieve and that the market distortions they introduce are kept to a minimum. All these provide the foundations upon which long-term growth in Pakistan can be possible.

APPENDIXES

Table A1: Economies in the ADB Multiregional Input–Output Database

ID	Code	Name	Region
1	AUS	Australia	East Asia and Pacific
2	AUT	Austria	Europe and Central Asia
3	BEL	Belgium	Europe and Central Asia
4	BGR	Bulgaria	Europe and Central Asia
5	BRA	Brazil	Latin America and the Caribbean
6	CAN	Canada	North America
7	SWI	Switzerland	Europe and Central Asia
8	PRC	People's Republic of China	East Asia and Pacific
9	CYP	Cyprus	Europe and Central Asia
10	CZE	Czech Republic	Europe and Central Asia
11	GER	Germany	Europe and Central Asia
12	DEN	Denmark	Europe and Central Asia
13	SPA	Spain	Europe and Central Asia
14	EST	Estonia	Europe and Central Asia
15	FIN	Finland	Europe and Central Asia
16	FRA	France	Europe and Central Asia
17	UKG	United Kingdom	Europe and Central Asia
18	GRC	Greece	Europe and Central Asia
19	HRV	Croatia	Europe and Central Asia
20	HUN	Hungary	Europe and Central Asia
21	INO	Indonesia	East Asia and Pacific
22	IND	India	South Asia
23	IRE	Ireland	Europe and Central Asia
24	ITA	Italy	Europe and Central Asia
25	JPN	Japan	East Asia and Pacific
26	KOR	Republic of Korea	East Asia and Pacific
27	LTU	Lithuania	Europe and Central Asia
28	LUX	Luxembourg	Europe and Central Asia
29	LVA	Latvia	Europe and Central Asia
30	MEX	Mexico	Latin America and the Caribbean
31	MLT	Malta	Middle East and North Africa
32	NET	Netherlands	Europe and Central Asia
33	NOR	Norway	Europe and Central Asia

ID	Code	Name	Region
34	POL	Poland	Europe and Central Asia
35	POR	Portugal	Europe and Central Asia
36	ROU	Romania	Europe and Central Asia
37	RUS	Russian Federation	Europe and Central Asia
38	SVK	Slovak Republic	Europe and Central Asia
39	SVN	Slovenia	Europe and Central Asia
40	SWE	Sweden	Europe and Central Asia
41	TUR	Turkey	Europe and Central Asia
42	TAP	Taipei,China	East Asia and Pacific
43	USA	United States	North America
44	BAN	Bangladesh	South Asia
45	MAL	Malaysia	East Asia and Pacific
46	PHI	Philippines	East Asia and Pacific
47	THA	Thailand	East Asia and Pacific
48	VIE	Viet Nam	East Asia and Pacific
49	KAZ	Kazakhstan	Europe and Central Asia
50	MON	Mongolia	East Asia and Pacific
51	SRI	Sri Lanka	South Asia
52	PAK	Pakistan	South Asia
53	FIJ	Fiji	East Asia and Pacific
54	LAO	Lao People's Democratic Republic	East Asia and Pacific
55	BRU	Brunei Darussalam	East Asia and Pacific
56	BHU	Bhutan	South Asia
57	KGZ	Kyrgyz Republic	Europe and Central Asia
58	CAM	Cambodia	East Asia and Pacific
59	MLD	Maldives	South Asia
60	NEP	Nepal	South Asia
61	SIN	Singapore	East Asia and Pacific
62	HKG	Hong Kong, China	East Asia and Pacific
63	ROW	Rest of the world	

ADB = Asian Development Bank.
Source: Asian Development Bank. Multiregional Input–Output Database (accessed 1 August 2021).

Table A2: Sectors in the ADB Multiregional Input–Output Database

ID	Name	Short Name	Code	ISIC 3.1
1	Agriculture, hunting, forestry and fishing	Agriculture	AHF	A–B
2	Mining and quarrying	Mining	MIN	C
3	Food, beverages and tobacco	Food & beverages	FBT	D15–16
4	Textiles and textile products	Textiles	TEX	D17–18
5	Leather, leather products and footwear	Leather	LTH	D19
6	Wood and products of wood and cork	Wood	WDC	D20
7	Pulp, paper, printing and publishing	Paper	PPP	D21–22
8	Coke, refined petroleum and nuclear fuel	Refined fuels	CRP	D23
9	Chemicals and chemical products	Chemicals	CCP	D24
10	Rubber and plastics	Rubber	RBP	D25
11	Other non-metallic mineral	Other minerals	ONM	D26
12	Basic metals and fabricated metal	Metals	MFM	D27–28
13	Machinery, not elsewhere classified	Other machinery	MCH	D29
14	Electrical and optical equipment	Electricals	EOE	D30–33
15	Transport equipment	Transport equipment	TRE	D34–35
16	Manufacturing, not elsewhere classified; recycling	Other manufacturing	MFG	D36–37
17	Electricity, gas and water supply	Utilities	UTL	E
18	Construction	Construction	CON	F
19	Sale and repair of motor vehicles and motorcycles; retail sale of fuel	Sale of motor vehicles	MTV	G50
20	Wholesale trade, except of motor vehicles and motorcycles	Wholesale trade	WST	G51
21	Retail trade and repair, except of motor vehicles and motorcycles	Retail trade & repair	RTR	G52
22	Hotels and restaurants	Hotels & restaurants	HRS	H
23	Inland transport	Inland transport	ITR	I60
24	Water transport	Water transport	WTR	I61
25	Air transport	Air transport	ATR	I62
26	Other supporting transport activities	Other transport services	OTR	I63
27	Post and telecommunications	Telecommunications	TEL	I64
28	Financial intermediation	Finance	FIN	J65–67
29	Real estate activities	Real estate	REA	K70
30	Renting of machinery & equipment and other business activities	Other business services	OBA	K71–74
31	Public administration and defence; compulsory social security	Public administration	PAD	L
32	Education	Education	EDU	M
33	Health and social work	Social work	HSW	N
34	Other community, social and personal services	Other personal services	OSV	O
35	Private households with employed persons	Private households	PHE	P

ADB = Asian Development Bank, ISIC = International Standard Industrial Classification.
Source: Asian Development Bank. Multiregional Input–Output Database (accessed 1 August 2021).

REFERENCES

P. Antràs and D. Chor. 2013. Organizing the Global Value Chain. *Econometrica*. 81 (6). pp. 2127–2204.

P. S. Armington. 1969. A Theory of Demand for Products Distinguished by Place of Production. *International Monetary Fund Staff Papers*. 16 (1). pp. 159–78.

Asian Development Bank (ADB). 2020a. *Country Partnership Strategy: Pakistan, 2021–2025—Lifting Growth, Building Resilience, Increasing Competitiveness*. Manila.

ADB. 2020b. *Pakistan: Reviving Growth Through Competitiveness*. Manila.

ADB. 2021. *Key Indicators for Asia and the Pacific 2021*. Manila.

B. Balassa. 1965. Trade Liberalisation and "Revealed" Comparative Advantage. *The Manchester School*. 33 (2). pp. 99–123.

R. Banga. 2014. Linking into Global Value Chains Is Not Sufficient: Do You Export Domestic Value Added Contents? *Journal of Economic Integration*. 29 (2). pp. 267–297.

D. Bartelme and Y. Gorodnichenko. 2015. Linkages and Economic Development. *NBER Working Paper*. No. 21251. Cambridge, MA: National Bureau of Economic Research.

T. Bayoumi, J. Lee, and S. Jayanthi. 2005. New Rates from New Weights. *IMF Working Paper*. No. WP/05/99. Washington, DC: International Monetary Fund.

T. Baysan, A. Panagariya, and N. Pitigala. 2006. Preferential Trading in South Asia. *World Bank Policy Research Working Paper*. No. 3813. Washington, DC: World Bank.

R. Bems and R. C. Johnson. 2017. Demand for Value Added and Value-Added Exchange Rates. *American Economic Journal: Macroeconomics*. 9 (4). pp. 45–90.

A. B. Bernard, J. B. Jensen, S. J. Redding, and P. K. Schott. 2007. Firms in International Trade. *Journal of Economic Perspectives*. 21 (3), pp. 105–130.

A. Borin and M. Mancini. 2019. Measuring What Matters in Global Value Chains and Value-Added Trade. *Policy Research Working Paper*. No. 8804. Washington, DC: World Bank.

S. Chatterjee and A. Subramanian. 2020. India's Export-Led Growth: Exemplar and Exception. *Ashoka Center for Economic Policy Working Paper*. No. 1. Sonipat, India: Ashoka University.

M. D. Chinn. 2006. A Primer on Real Effective Exchange Rates: Determinants, Overvaluation, Trade Flows and Competitive Devaluation. *Open Economies Review*. 51 (1). pp. 115–43.

D. Dollar, B. Khan, and P. Pei. 2019. Should High Domestic Value Added in Exports Be an Objective of Policy? In World Bank and World Trade Organization. *Global Value Chain Development Report 2019: Technological Innovation, Supply Chain Trade, and Workers in a Globalized World*. Washington, DC: World Bank.

H. Escaith and S. Inomata. 2013. Geometry of Global Value Chains in East Asia: The Role of Industrial Networks and Trade Policies. In D. K. Elms and P. Low, eds. *Global Value Chains in a Changing World*. Geneva: World Trade Organization. pp. 135–157.

European Commission. 2008. *Eurostat Manual of Supply, Use and Input-Output Tables*. Luxembourg.

J. A. Frankel. 1997. *Regional Trading Blocs in the World Economic System*. Washington, DC: Peterson Institute for International Economics.

J. A. Frankel and D. Romer. 1999. Does Trade Cause Growth? *American Economic Review*. 89 (3). pp. 379–399.

S. Giglioli, G. Giovannetti, E. Marvasi, and A. Vivoli. 2021. The Resilience of Global Value Chains During the Covid-19 Pandemic: The Case of Italy. *UniFI DISEI Working Papers – Economics*. No. 07/2021. Florence, Italy: Università degli Studi Firenze Dipartimento di Scienze per L'Economia e L'Impresa.

Government of Japan, Ministry of Economy, Trade and Industry (METI). 2011. *White Paper on International Economy and Trade*. Supplementary Notes.

D. Hummels, J. Ishii, and K. M. Yi. 2001. The Nature and Growth of Vertical Specialization in World Trade. *Journal of International Economics*. 54 (1). pp. 75–96.

S. Inomata. 2017. Analytical Frameworks for Global Value Chains: An Overview. In World Bank. *Global Value Chain Development Report 2017: Measuring and Analyzing the Impact of GVCs on Economic Development*. Washington, DC. pp. 15–35.

International Monetary Fund (IMF). 2019. *World Economic Outlook, October 2019: Global Manufacturing Downturn, Rising Trade Barriers*. Washington, DC.

IMF. World Economic Outlook Database: April 2021 edition (accessed 1 August 2021).

O. Itskhoki. 2020. The Story of the Real Exchange Rate. *NBER Working Paper*. No. 28225. Cambridge, MA: National Bureau of Economic Research.

C. I. Jones. 2011. Intermediate Goods and Weak Links in the Theory of Economic Development. *American Economic Journal: Macroeconomics*. 3 (2). pp. 1–28.

Kearney. 2021. *Global Pandemic Roils 2020 Reshoring Index, Shifting Focus from Reshoring to Right-Shoring*. Chicago, IL.

R. Koopman, Z. Wang, and S. Wei. 2014. Tracing Value-Added and Double Counting in Gross Exports. *American Economic Review*. 104 (2). pp. 459–494.

N. Limão. 2016. Preferential Trade Agreements. *NBER Working Paper*. No. 22138. Cambridge, MA: National Bureau of Economic Research.

B. McCaig and N. Pavcnik. 2018. Export Markets and Labor Allocation in a Low-Income Country. *American Economic Review*. 108 (7). pp. 1899–1941.

V. Mercer-Blackman, A. Foronda, and M. J. Mariasingham. 2017. Using Input–Output Analysis Framework to Explain Economic Diversification and Structural Transformation in Bangladesh. *ADB Economics Working Paper Series*. No. 513. Manila: Asian Development Bank.

J. Nasir. 2020. The Tariff Tripod of Pakistan: Protection, Export Promotion, and Revenue Generation. *PIDE Working Papers*. No. 2020:6. Islamabad: Pakistan Institute of Development Economics.

S. Patel, Z. Wang, and S. Wei. 2019. Global Value Chains and Effective Exchange Rates at the Country-Sector Level. *Journal of Money, Credit and Banking*. 51 (1). pp. 7–42.

W. F. Shughart. 2008. Industrial Concentration. In D. R. Henderson, ed. *Concise Encyclopedia of Economics*. 2nd ed. Indianapolis, IN: Library of Economics and Liberty.

State Bank of Pakistan. 2021. *The State of Pakistan's Economy 2020-21: First Quarterly Report of the Board of Directors*. Karachi.

I. Stephens. 1967. *Pakistan*. 3rd ed. New York: Frederick A. Praeger.

J. E. Stiglitz. 1996. Some Lessons from the East Asian Miracle. *The World Bank Research Observer*. 11 (2). pp. 151–177.

M. P. Thomas. 2018. Impact of Services Trade on Economic Growth and Current Account Balance: Evidence from India. *Journal of International Trade and Economic Development*. 28 (3). pp. 331–347.

M. P. Timmer, E. Dietzenbacher, B. Los, R. Stehrer, and G. J. de Vries. 2015. An Illustrated User Guide to the World Input-Output Database: The Case of Global Automotive Production. *Review of International Economics*. 23 (3). pp. 575–605.

Z. Wang, S. Wei, X. Yu, and K. Zhu. 2017a. Measures of Participation in Global Value Chains and Global Business Cycles. *NBER Working Paper*. No. 23222. Cambridge, MA: National Bureau of Economic Research.

Z. Wang, S. Wei, X. Yu, and K. Zhu. 2017b. Characterizing Global Value Chains: Production Length and Upstreamness. *NBER Working Paper*. No. 23261. Cambridge, MA: National Bureau of Economic Research.

S. A. Wolpert. 2004. *A New History of India*. 7th ed. Oxford, United Kingdom: Oxford University Press.

World Bank. 2020a. *Islamic Republic of Pakistan: Leveling the Playing Field—Systematic Country Diagnostic*. Washington, DC.

World Bank. 2020b. *Global Economic Prospects, January 2020: Slow Growth, Policy Challenges*. Washington, DC.

World Trade Organization (WTO). 2011a. *World Trade Report 2011—The WTO and Preferential Trade Agreements: From Co-Existence to Coherence*. Geneva.

WTO. 2011b. *Trade Patterns and Global Value Chains in East Asia: From Trade in Goods to Trade in Tasks*. Geneva.